# IT'S NOT EASY TO MARRY AN ELEPHANT

# IT'S NOT EASY TO MARRY AN ELEPHANT

## And Other Fables

*By Beatrice Chernuchin Schuman*

*Illustrated by Roland Wolff*

FREDERICK FELL PUBLISHERS, INC.

*New York, New York*

398.245
Schuman

Copyright © 1982 by Beatrice Chernuchin Schuman
Illustrations copyright © 1982 by Roland Wolff

All rights reserved. No part of this work covered by the copyright may be reproduced or used in any form or by any means—graphic, electronic, or mechanical, including photocopying, recording, taping, or information storage and retrieval systems—without permission of the publisher.

*For information address:*
FREDERICK FELL PUBLISHERS, INC.
386 Park Avenue South
New York, New York 10016

Library of Congress Catalog Card Number: 81-68909
International Standard Book Number: 0-8119-0436-9

Manufactured in the United States of America
1 2 3 4 5 6 7 8 9 0

Published simultaneously in Canada by Fitzhenry & Whiteside Limited, Toronto

**FOR JULIE ANN EBENSTEIN**
*With Love*

# CONTENTS

# CONTENTS

# IT'S NOT EASY TO
# MARRY AN ELEPHANT

Ellie was an elephant and she never forgot what her mother had taught her: The best way of life was the married way. But it's not easy to marry an elephant.

She met Foxie on the plains. "Who gave an elephant such a name?" she asked.

"I move fast and swift. So my folks gave me that name."

Fast and swift to Ellie meant he would move fast and swift to the wedding bower, so she rubbed trunks with him.

"Let's . . . ," said Foxy.

"I'm saving it for the elephant I will love and wed."

"But how will I know we are physically compatible if we don't try each other out?"

Ellie agreed to the compatibility test and she rated as high as a circus performer. Foxy was so pleased that his trumpeting sounds could be heard a mile away.

"So when are we getting married, Foxy?" asked Ellie.

"Do you believe in God?" he asked.

"Of course," she squealed. "What is there not to believe in?"

"What God?"

"God of the Plain, of course," she replied.

"I believe in the God of India," he said.

"So I can believe in the God of India, too. Let's get married."

"But my mother believes in the God of India. And she believes that once you believe in the God of the Plain, you are a Plain God Believer. And I can't hurt my mother. She's very old. And sick. It would kill her if I married a Plain God Believer. When she dies we'll get married."

So Ellie waited for the day. She prepared a trousseau. And she and Foxy remained lovers.

"May your mother live till a hundred and twenty, but I hear that the life expectancy of elephants is fifty to sixty—and your mother is already eighty."

"I believe that long life comes from not aggravating yourself, and I make sure that my mother doesn't get any aggravation."

Ellie's hide was beginning to bleach due to advancing age. She found she couldn't run so fast. And she wanted little ones. But she had patience. Mama couldn't live forever. One beautiful day she would die.

And one day, Mama tripped over a mongoose and broke her hip. And all of Foxy's screaming and all the efforts of the troop to lift her to her feet were of no avail.

Mama died.

"All your nudging can't bring Mama back," squealed Ellie, "but we can get married and have a little one to replace her, and she can send her soul to this earthly world to become the soul of our little one."

"A wonderful idea," boomed Foxy. "A beautiful idea."

Ellie brought Foxy to her lair to show him her trousseau.

10

"Wonderful. Beautiful," he roared. "Just fit for a home for our baby elephant who will have the soul of my mother."

"Let's get the invitations out," squealed Ellie.

"For what?"

"For our wedding."

"After we have our home."

"Any old lean-to at the side of a tree will do for me."

"But not for our baby elephant who will carry the soul of my mother. We need the best."

"To get the best will take plenty of timber. It takes time."

"I know. It takes time. But we elephants have a long life expectancy. I have time and you have time, and when we can buy that home with all our own timber, we'll get married . . ."

---

### MORAL

Mothers grow old and die, but promises go on forever.

---

# LUCKY

Ducky was a plucky duck. And Lucky Duck was lucky. He made bulletproof vests for sitting ducks, and was a master at his craft.

"You bring me luck," he said to Ducky.

"It's your skill that makes you successful," she said.

Whether it was Lucky's skill that made him successful or the luck waves that Ducky sent him, she enjoyed sharing some of the rewards of his success. Oh, how she loved going dressed in all her finery to The Songbird's Opera. It would be hard for her to name her favorite. *Madame Butterfly*? Or *At The Boar's Head*? *Oberon* or *Orpheus*? *The Firebird*? Or *The Fairy Queen*? The nights the Ducks went to the opera were the most important nights of Ducky's life.

Her life with Lucky was not easy. Living with a successful bird never is. There was gossip.

"I hear you're always chasing after chicks," Ducky said.

"Of course. I'm trying to get the business."

"Hortense has laid some eggs. Rumor has it that you were the last male seen with her."

"Now are you going to believe ugly rumors or are you going to believe me?"

Lucky began to bring her less and less grain.

But she understood. It takes a lot of grain to be a swain.

He spent less and less time with her.

And she understood. It takes time, too.

"I'm going to wear my new black spangled dress with the red embroidered Mandarin coat opening night, Lucky," she said.

"The opera? Didn't I mention that I didn't renew our subscription? We have to economize somewhere, you know."

"But Lucky . . . ," she pleaded.

"You know there's a recession," he said.

"It means so much to me," she said.

"We can't spend grain on that culture garbage. We have to build a little nest egg."

"Not even a half-subscription?"

"Not even a half-subscription."

"Or maybe a quarter-subscription?"

"Not even a quarter-subscription."

"How about once in a while?"

"No. And that's final," said Lucky.

"Final?"

"Final."

Ducky could understand a lot, but not this. More ducks than ever were buying vests. Because of the recession, poachers were out in full force. And where other than at the opera could she wear her two-piece hand-painted gown with the petal skirt, and where other than at the opera could she wear her orchid-sequined blouson? and where other than at the opera could she hear the beautiful music she loved?

It was clear to Ducky that she had to go to the opera. And like any duck who wants something badly enough, she found a way.

She dug up the grain she had put away for an emergency. She couldn't think of any emergency that could be more of an emergency than this.

"A subscription for the opera," she requested of the ticket-seller.

"How many?" he asked.

How many? She hadn't thought about how lonely it would be to go to the opera all dressed up and have no duck to share the excitement with her. "Two. Of course," she said.

Ducky went to the opera house on opening night and waited for an interesting-looking male who, upon asking for a ticket, would be told that the opera was sold out. She invited the most attractive one to be her guest. And she had a pleasant time indeed. And Ducky went to all the operas to which she had subscribed with a different escort each time.

Gossip tattled to Lucky. "So your mate has taken many lovers. I guess you're not so lucky any more."

Lucky's head drooped and his eyes resembled those of a wounded bird. "I guess I'm not. I'd better philander a little myself and teach her a lesson."

And Lucky was luckier than ever. He was no longer bothered with qualms of conscience.

## MORAL

**How lucky can you get!**

# MAXWELL FIGHTS BACK

Chichi was a chipmunk who was determined to be in the chips, so she pursued Maxwell, artist and scion of a wealthy chipmunk. But Maxwell knew his own heart and he had heart only for Gretchen and he wed sweet Gretchen.

Their wedding was more than Chichi could bear. She went to another land where she hoped she would be more successful. And indeed she was. There she wed Morgan Mor-chipmunk and fell into more chips than even she had dreamed of. Morgan Mor-chipmunk is, of course, one of *the* Mor-chipmunks, whose thoroughbred minihorses have won many a purse in the Contucky Derbies.

The doors of chipmunk society were thrown open to the Mor-chipmunks. Chichi's face was often on the pages of the *Chipmunk Social Times*. Chipmunks young and old bought Chippie Youth Creams because Madame Mor-chipmunk claimed that the creams gave her the coat of a mink.

To this new land, too, came Maxwell with his Gretchen. Maxwell had painted many paintings, and he felt that in this land chipmunks would buy them.

16

**r.**

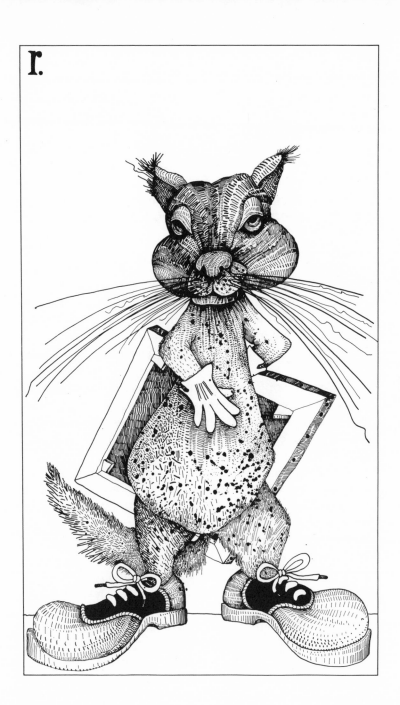

"Let's visit Chichi," said Gretchen. "It will be good for us to talk with her of her life in this land and we can tell her, too, about her old friends in our native land."

She called Chichi.

"I am busy on Monday, Tuesday, and Friday. And on Wednesday and Saturday, of course, I will preside at the auction for the benefit of Aged Racehorses. Why don't you call me after lunch and before tea someday. If nothing important comes up, you may visit me and watch the races on the telly."

Well!

Gretchen wept. And Maxwell wept because his Gretchen wept. They felt beaten, thrown to the ground. No matter that in their own country they were chipmunks of note. "We are so low—no chipmunks can be lower than us," said Gretchen. "We are so low that we cannot earn even a luncheon with a chipmunk from our native country."

Maxwell could not bear to see his Gretchen hurt. He was ordinarily a mild-tempered chipmunk who had no taste to fight his way in the battles of the forest. He was usually a dove, but when provoked he could become a hawk.

"Have no worry, shatzi; have no worry, my poopkin. One day soon Chichi will call on you," he said.

The next day Maxwell called Chichi. "I believe your cause is truly a great cause. I believe that Aged Racehorses should not be forgotten. I would like to support your charity, so I will donate a painting for your auction." Maxwell was hardly concerned about the care of Aged Racehorses. But Maxwell was deeply concerned about the feelings and sensitivities of Gretchen. And for this cause Maxwell was eager to donate a painting.

"We thank you," said Chichi. "All contributions must be delivered through the service entrance no earlier than 6:00 A.M. on Monday and no later than 6:07."

# MAXWELL FIGHTS BACK

Maxwell was determined to paint a painting that no creature could forget. He prepared himself for this painting: He ate rattlesnake meat and rotted entrails to produce for him a nightmare and oh, what a scary nightmare it produced. He recalled as much of it as he could use and brushed it on his canvas. The morbid purples, the shadows of the night. The beady eyes of the fox. The stealthy walk of the panther ready to spring. The jaws of the rhinoceros. The claws of the falcon. One elegantly clad animal, the composite unmistakably. . . .

"I bid ten thousand chips," said Chichi, her voice more a gasp than a whisper. Hers was the first and last bid—at the price that might have been paid for a Monard or a Dauphin—but no wonder.

That evening Chichi paid the Maxwells the visit Max had promised his Gretchen. Clamped in her jaws was her newly acquired portrait. In her enraged mood her portrait was not too unlike her.

"You weasel!" she shrieked. And she ripped the portrait to pieces with her claws, spat in a most inelegant fashion, and slinked away.

## MORAL

**A dove when provoked can become a hawk.**

# I'LL TELL THE WORLD

In the foundation of a big white house, on a country lane at the edge of a forest, lived a colony of ants. They spent their days chewing away at the foundation of the house.

Super-Ant, an ant of a more enterprising breed, ambled by one day. He could see that this colony was heading for big trouble. "When the owners of the house find out what you are up to," he said, "it will be the fumigators for you. Wait! Don't go away. Listen. You can find a bump on a log and be a bump on a bump on a log like a pack of idlers, or you can participate in my project."

Super-Ant explained: "There's a big demand for wormy chestnut wood now. But the prices are getting so high that the average homeowners can't afford it. Right down the lane is a wonderful pine forest. I can train you to eat away at the pinewood. I can get a good price for it on the market, but it still would be lower than the price of the wormy chestnut. You do a job on it; I know I can sell plenty; and I will compensate you well for your labors."

The ants conferred. They weren't happy to hear they were one step ahead of the exterminator. Pinewood might

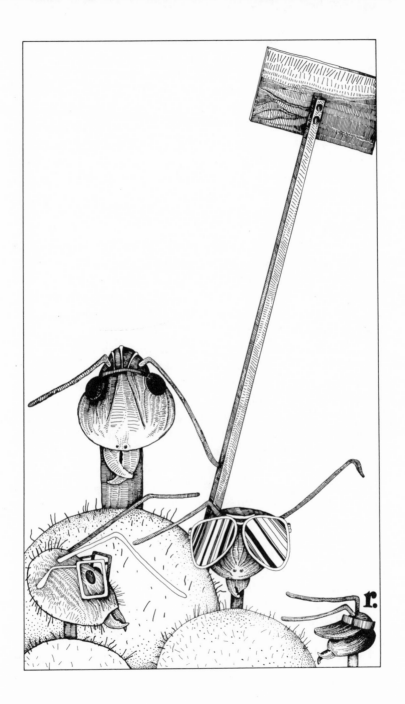

be a delicious change. And compensation, too? The ants all agreed to work on the pinewood.

They went to work enthusiastically. They had never done such work before, yet they were most artistic in chewing out their designs. They made oval holes and round holes, diamonds and hexagons. Their work was so artistic that when the lumberers came to make their purchases, one lumberer was heard to say, "This will take over the market. It is even more beautiful than the wormy chestnut."

The ants were happy. They found that eating the pinewood could satisfy the most epicurean among them. And they were pleased, too, with their compensation and their time off for skiing and hunting. And no worry about the fumigator, now that they knew they had the fumigator to worry about.

Super-Ant was happy and very proud. He had taken a colony of ants who did no useful work and had created a constructive occupation for them. He had developed a new product for the market. What an example this would be for other colonies who couldn't find anything constructive to do! He would like to tell the world about it.

He called the "What's New" desk of *The International Ant.* They sent a reporter. The story was placed on the front page where no reader could miss it.

And no reader missed the story.

Organizer read it.

He called a meeting of the pinewood workers. "Where have you ants been for the last century? Don't you know that every worker should be organized so he can fight for what he needs?"

"I have everything I need," said Meek.

"Do you have two toilets for every ant? And indoor and outdoor showers for the dry season? And what about a sunshade? Does each and every ant have a sunshade that can be rolled up or down as is necessary? Three sweet peas an hour! And you call that compensation! If you join our organization we will get you everything."

The ants liked the way things were but if things could be better, then why not?

The ants joined the organization.

They made their demands.

Everything was agreed to but the sunshade clause.

Strike!

Some of the ants got hungry and went back to chewing at the foundation of the big white house. Others went to chew on random logs. Some waited out the strike until they got their sunshades and then went back to work.

With the cost of the new benefits, however, the selling price of the "wormy" pine became higher than that of the wormy chestnut. And most of the customers went back to buying the wormy chestnut. And things are no better for any of the ants today.

**MORAL**

**Some benefits, in the long run, are not beneficial.**

# NUTS AND HONEY

Aunt Fanny was a bear, a bear with a heart so big that when Papa Bear was felled by a rotted elm and his widow was mowed down by a hunter's gun, she tried to be mama and papa, as well as auntie, to Little Moe. And when Little Moe became Big Moe and took himself a bride, she did a mama's job of welcoming Flo into the family.

"Make yourself comfortable. I have a treat for you," she said. And she served her treat. She didn't tell Moe and Flo that she had been up since dawn gathering hazelnuts. She didn't tell them how hard it was for her to crack all the nuts, or how many nests she had to rip open to get the honey, or how tired she was standing over the hot kettle all day stirring the mixture. She didn't tell them, of course, what it did to her sinuses when she added the ginger, or how difficult it was for her to roll the candy into flat sheets and cut the sheets into small pieces with her claws.

Aunt Fanny didn't tell them any of these unpleasant things because when she served the hazelnut candy, Flo always gurgled, "It's delicious. I'm crazy about it." Aunt Fanny didn't mind putting all this effort into making the candy. Really. Well, not too much, for the pleasure she gave to her niece and nephew was worth all the trouble she went to in preparing the candy.

Every Wednesday evening, Flo and Moe called on Aunt Fanny. And every Wednesday evening Aunt Fanny had the hazelnut candy waiting for them. And whatever candy they didn't finish eating while they visited, Aunt Fanny wrapped and gave them to take to their den.

On a Wednesday, three years, five months, and fourteen days after their wedding, Moe and Flo, as usual, called on Aunt Fanny. That Wednesday was the day that Moe had complained to Flo that she slept all day and didn't even leave the den to bring in a piece of fish. Aunt Fanny served the hazelnut candy.

This time Flo didn't say it was delicious. She didn't say she was crazy about it. This time she said nothing.

"It's a little hard today?" Aunt Fanny asked.

Flo shook her head.

"I had it on the fire for a long time. Maybe I burned it?"

Flo shook her head again.

"I know it's the end of the nut season and the nuts are dried out a little?"

"No . . ."

"Then what's wrong? It's too nutty?"

And now Flo roared as loud as any bear could roar, "I HATE HAZELNUTS."

## NUTS AND HONEY

And Aunt Fanny never made hazelnut candy for Moe and Flo again.

## MORAL

Better communication may keep a bear from going nuts.

# CROW

Calvin was a crow—a good enough crow, as crows go, but not good enough for Clarissa.

"You swallow everything that every bird gives you," Clarissa cawed. "It's enough to make me want to regurgitate. I know Gilda Crow told you she would teach you how to arrange oak leaves to make them look like a rainbow, but you didn't have to bite her line like any poor fish. When the God of All Creatures gave out brains, he sure missed you. And look at you. You're not black-black as a crow should be, but God help you, in some spots you're grey, and it hurts me to say this, but there are some places where you're almost white—caw, caw, caw. Caw, I should have married Mr. Ittlecrow. His fledglings sleep on maple leaves and your poor babes sleep on a bed of needles."

Calvin hopped to the TV perch and turned the sound of "Bird Man" on as loud as he could. Alas, it did not drown out Clarissa's voice. She turned her own volume louder and cawed as loud as she could.

"And how many rodents did you bring home today?" she cawed. "And how much corn? *You* want to rule the roost but you hardly bring in a flea."

"Crick, crick, crick-crick-crick," whimpered Calvin. Now he sounded more like a cricket than a crow. Ah, if he could but find some sap oozing from a maple tree to give him the strength to withstand her tirade, he thought. But he didn't even have the energy to look for a gnat.

His good friends wondered why Calvin didn't go bye, bye, blackbird. Or migrate with a more peaceful mate. Harvey, one of the flock, asked him why he stayed with Clarissa.

"I think she might have swallowed some bramble thorns today," he explained. "She's usually not like this. You only hear her nagging caws, but when she's with her friends she always warbles, and quite musically at that." And he added, "But she'll be okay soon, I know. At least I have to give her a fair chance."

Calvin felt that she could change, that someday the good that was in her would come out—the good that he felt was in every bird.

And, one blue Sunday—"Dummy, I told you to french the worms for tonight's stew," Clarissa screeched. "And don't give me any of your beak that it's female's work."

Calvin was abject. "What can I do to please you?" he asked. "I have tried everything. Shall I stand on my head?"

Clarissa's big black eyes lit up. "That's the most intelligent thing you've said in a long time. Yes, Bird-brain, stand on your head."

Well, Calvin was a bird who wanted peace. And Calvin was a bird who would do anything to get peace. And Calvin was a bird who believed that the only way he could get a feather was to give a wing. And he believed

that if he stood on his head, maybe he would crush his brains. And that if he crushed his brains, maybe he would die. And if he died, maybe Clarissa would be sorry. At the very least, he would have peace.

And queek, queek, a little tear rolled down Calvin's left eye because he was so sorry for Clarissa, who was soon to be very sorry that he had died. And queek, queek, a tear rolled down his right eye because he was so sorry for himself that he was soon to die. And then the tears rolled down both his eyes because he was so sorry that he was sad.

He kicked up his skinny little left leg. And then he kicked up his skinny little right leg. And he did a back-flip, landing on his head.

Happily, Calvin did not crush his brain. The worst thing that happened, or from a different point of view, the best thing that happened, was that he flipped out a bit. He got very lightheaded. He got mischievous. He kicked his feet about up in the air. "Fun! Fun! Fee, fi, fun! Little Calvin wants to run! Wheeeeeee!" he chuckled gleefully.

And then he thought about Clarissa. He knew he couldn't have fun without Clarissa's approval. He looked at Clarissa. But wait. What was Clarissa doing? To Calvin's bird mind, his perception of Clarissa from the position he was in was that *Clarissa* was standing on her head. He took a good look at her. He took a very good look. Why, bottoms up, she looks like any old crow! he thought. And surely no bird to fear.

He sang (*pianissimo* at first):

The old black crow, she ain't what she used to be,
Ain't what she used to be, ain't what she used to be—

And he crescendoed to a *forte*:

# CROW

The old black crow, she ain't what she used to be,
Many long years ago, ho, ho.

Now Calvin was really getting playful. He found a ring from an empty beer can and ceremoniously placed it on Clarissa's left claw. "With this ring, my beloved, I thee crown queen of the drones," he said.

"You look like a cuckoo, you weasel," Clarissa screeched. "Where are you going?"

"And you, you shrew, you don't look like a swan. Where? I'm off to see the wizard, the wonderful wizard of Was. And let me hear silence from you, you old bag of wind."

And at that moment, Clarissa did indeed seem like a windbag. She swallowed and swallowed and swallowed the air. And as she swallowed, her face blew up. And her body blew up, and blew up, and blew up and blew up until, alas, it burst. It burst into a thousand tiny pieces that were flung far and wide to the branches of the sapodilla trees.

But have no fear—fear not at all. Clarissa is not gone; nor is she, nor will she ever be forgotten. She lives today in the sapodilla trees, and if you go to Randy's Candy Store, you can buy part of her essence in a little licorice gum ball. How do I know she's there? Well, get a gum ball at Andy's, and chew. And then blow bubbles till they burst with a roar, or, shall I say, a caw. And the roar, or, if you will, the caw, is Clarissa's voice. And the sap, which is made into gum, is part of Clarissa's essence. And Clarissa is being chewed, and she can no longer chew Calvin, or any bird, for that matter. (Oh my, how the mighty can fall!)

And what happened to Calvin?

Calvin went swimming in a bottle of tequila,
And then flew away, flew off to Manila.

## CROW

He flew as the crow flies,
He flew free and easy,
And ate yellow corn—
Without Clarissa life was breezy.

## MORAL

A crow doesn't have to eat crow.

# THE CHEETAHS

In a remote corner of a forest lived a tribe of cheetahs. Swift of foot, they captured game, more game than they had need for. Their brains were highly developed; they were the brainiest of the animals who lived in the woods.

"Why not exchange our surplus antelopes for some of the goodies we lack in our homeland?" suggested one of the brainiest. And they did. They exchanged their antelopes for chariots that had motors, and were able to move about without using their legs. They exchanged their antelopes for pipes that could bring the water to them and for magical objects that could make their waste disappear into the ground. And they cleared their corner of the forest to build roads on which to drive their chariots, and to construct houses in which to keep their magical objects, as well as provide shelter from the rain and the hot summer sun.

They felt good. "We are the chosen ones," they said.

And since they felt they were the chosen ones they declared, "All cheetahs are brothers." And since they felt they were the chosen ones, and the brainiest by far, they went further and said all cheetahs have rights, and being as brainy as they were, they put their beliefs in a formal bill.

They called it the Bill of Rights, which stated therein that all cheetahs had the right to the pursuit of happiness and that every cheetah had the right to go before the chosen chosen one—who was chosen in an election of the chosen ones—if his pursuit of happiness was obstructed by any other cheetah.

And they felt good.

"I don't feel very good," Compassion Cheetah told herself. "I don't even feel good. I feel bad." Compassion regularly checked her feelings each hour. "The bluebirds no longer nest in our woodlands. We have cleared their wild fruit away. Without hearing their cheerful call or their sweet warbling song, I cannot be happy."

Compassion studied the Bill of Rights. Yes, her rights had been infringed upon. Article I, Line 1, Section 1, said that all cheetahs had the right to the pursuit of happiness. "I have a right . . . ," Compassion confirmed. "I cannot be happy if I do not hear the chirps and twitters of the bluebird coming from the wild fruit trees." And she checked the Bill of Rights further and found that Article I, Line 4, Section 2 said that every cheetah had the right to go before the chosen chosen one if his pursuit of happiness was obstructed by any other cheetah. She felt good. A wrong would be righted. She would go before the chosen chosen one. "I will tell him that the bluebirds should have a bill of rights, too. In any case, my rights have been infringed upon."

"I have an urgent matter to discuss with you," she wrote the chosen chosen one. "I would like to see you."

"Put it in a letter," the secretary to the secretary of the chosen chosen one wrote back.

Compassion wrote another letter. She wrote of the sad infringement of her right.

This time, neither the secretary to the secretary, nor the secretary, nor the chosen chosen one, nor any chosen one answered her letter.

Compassion checked the Bill of Rights again. She read Article I, Line 4, Section 2 again. "Every cheetah has

the right to go before the chosen one if his pursuit of happiness is obstructed by any other cheetah."

She would go directly to the chosen chosen one. She would knock on his door and he would see that the bluebirds would again come in all their splendor to the trees that would replace their roads and houses.

She came to the iron gate in front of the big white house of the chosen chosen one.

"I have an urgent matter to discuss with the chosen chosen one," she told a guard at the gate.

"Put it in a letter," said the guard.

"But I put it in a letter," said Compassion, "and I got no reply."

"Put it in a letter," said the guard again.

The chosen chosen one would understand. She had to see him. She pushed the guard aside. Eight guards came to the aid of the guard of the gate. There were two guards who held each limb and one who held her mouth so none could hear her plea for her pursuit of happiness.

They put her in a cage—the charge: Illegal entry and attempted assassination of the chosen chosen one. When cheetahs pass her cage they say, "Look at Crazy Compassion."

**MORAL**

**Who ever said the pursuit promised the real thing?**

# THE OTHER

Boo, the baboon went to the end of the feed line at the community picnic.

"Leave a space for latecomers," said Foxie.

Boo smiled a self-effacing smile and turned around to walk a little further so he could leave the space he had been asked to leave. "What a nerd that Boo is," he heard the fox say to Wolfie.

Boo could tell from Foxie's expression that being a nerd wasn't something to be proud of. But what was a nerd? He always believed he was a baboon, but maybe he wasn't one at all. And maybe that was the reason he was often pushed aside, excluded, passed over, threatened. "Pardon me, Foxie. If you don't mind, I would like to apologize for disturbing you—and may I thank you in advance, but I heard you call me a nerd. What is a nerd?"

"Get away from me, boy, you're bothering me," said Foxie.

# THE OTHER

"Psst," whispered Wolfie, "if you really want to know, ask Crock Crocodile. She's one. She can tell you."

Boo knew that no creature bothered with Crock, she with her crocodile tears. Everything she clacked her jaws about was a crock. Boo couldn't see what he had in common with this inferior creature, but if she could help him understand what a nerd was, then perhaps he could understand better what he was. He had to know.

"A nerd?" said Crock. "Why ask me? Ask one who is one. May I direct you to Crybaby Coyote?"

Boo wasn't eager to talk to Crybaby. Crybaby yelped. He whined. He was always complaining. Surely he had nothing in common with that old howler.

"Sorry, pal. I can't help you," said Crybaby. "You should talk to Crawly. He's a first-rate nerd."

That caterpillar? He was contemptible, undesirable, a worthless worm, and yellow, too. But Boo had his mission. He wouldn't give up.

He went to Crawly, who sent him to Smelly (that skunk's deodorant never worked), who sent him to Scaredy (the cat who always ran away from a fight), who sent him to Gawky Goose, who sent him to Silly Lamb, who sent him to Dodo Bird, whom Boo could not track down.

But he no longer needed to find Dodo for the answer came to him just as he was being harassed by a flea. "Why, I know what a nerd is," he said with the excitement that comes of having made a discovery. "A nerd is—the other one." And then he concluded with satisfaction, "If it's the other one, then it can't, of course, be me."

And so Boo was able to live with himself, believing he was a baboon with all the same qualities as the best of his breed. And he went on being pushed aside, excluded, passed over, threatened by his fellow creatures, and remained, as always, a nerd.

## MORAL

Know thyself, nerd.

# THE HOGS

There lived, in a land not too far away, a drift of hogs. They had a reputation for being intelligent creatures, but they would swallow almost anything.

High promised them that if he were elected they would live high on the hog. Higher promised them that if he were elected, they would live higher. They elected Higher and they got more potatoes, but they had to give a good deal of them back to the government. It took a lot of potatoes to run the government.

The hogs grunted. There didn't seem to be much more they could do about it. Another election would be coming around soon and maybe things would get better. Oh, if they could only live off the fat of the land.

One day, some groundhogs were snooping about the governor's office when they uncovered some irregularities. They squealed. "Something's not kosher on Capitol Hill," they said. There was a scandal.

"We'll vote the swine out," said some.

"One politician's no better than another," said others.

"I won't vote at all," was heard from a few.

Longview was running as an independent. "Vote for me," he said.

# THE HOGS

"Where did you come from?" snorted a warthog. "I never saw you hanging around the wards. You never ran for office. You're just a pig in a poke."

"Let me tell you who I am," said Longview. He explained that he had started as a poor potato-digger and that he had made millions in farming. "I want to do something for my brothers. I feel called upon to do what I have proven I can do—make a big organization work. I will cut taxes without cutting down the services. The aged, the sick, and the helpless will still be taken care of. I will serve only one term if elected and then I will return to my own farm."

This was a new approach. And new promises: Cut taxes. And no cuts in service. There were enough voters who were against Higher's party and enough against High's to give Longview the votes necessary to elect him to office.

True to his promise, taxes were cut 25 percent; the hogs were able to keep 25 percent more of their potatoes; the budget was cut without cutting down the services; the aged, the sick, the helpless were still taken care of—but 50 percent of the warthogs were fired.

"Our jobs! We demand our jobs! That has always been our reward for our political work," squawked the warthogs.

"You'll have to dig for your own potatoes," said Longview. "There will be no more sinecures."

"We'll run you out of office."

"No need to—I'm leaving after this term."

They tried to sling mud at him, but none of it stuck until one sorry day when he expressed his private belief that boars were more equal than sows, and later said that they owed no goats who were too stupid to make a good deal, an extra share of potatoes. The whole constituency seemed to turn against him then.

## THE HOGS

At the next election, one party or another was elected and things went back to the way they were before Longview took office. All the good he had done was forgotten.

But this story has a happy ending, for one day Longview got hoof-and-mouth disease and went to hog heaven. Councilmen, mayors, senators, governors, and everyday, ordinary hogs came to pay homage. He was eulogized by the most prestigious. And on his tombstone was engraved, 'Here lies a truly altruistic hog.'

**MORAL**

**Some have to wait for heaven to get their reward.**

# KING
# OF THE JUNGLE

Hippo was a clumsy, slow-moving fellow. When he reached his sixth birthday he said, "Mama, I'd like to be king of the jungle."

"Drink your milk," said Mama. "Don't you know the lion is king of the jungle? But," she added, "you can be anything you want to be."

"Build a better people-trap," said Papa, "and the animal world will beat a path to your door."

"God forbid! All you have to do is trap a person and you'll be shot dead," said Mama.

"Work up ninety-nine percent sweat and roll in the mud a little and you can be anything. Even a king," said Papa.

So Hippo sweated. And he rolled in the mud. And he believed he could be anything he wanted to be. And he believed he'd better not build a people-trap or he'd get shot. But he thought a little charge wouldn't hurt anybody. And a lot of work might make him a king.

He took vitamin pills to give him more energy. He studied 'rate times time equals distance' and he learned

how to get electrical energy into the fences. He wired the jungle fences and used the power he got from the waterfalls to give the fences a charge.

Now Hippo was ready. He informed the curator of the Museum of Natural History that for fifty bananas a head he would give their safari group a show. The curator arranged to have a museum group come to the jungle and see The Performing Pantomimists and he promised Bananas On Delivery.

Hippo passed out circulars in the jungle:

Come to the Safari of the Museum of Natural History. The people will give a special performance. A shocker that has more laughs than a barrel of monkeys. Admission: 25 bananas. Admission for Dodos: 100 bananas.

"A humdinger"–*The Audubon News*
"A four-star show"–*The African Muse*
"Don't miss"–*The People's Hunter*

For a play that had not been seen by any creature, the quotes were pretty good. All the animals of the jungle came. There were elephants and giraffes, hippopotamuses and lions, rhinoceroses and camels, zebras, ocelots, and open-billed storks, to mention a few.

"Now a small request. Do you want the people to put on a good show?" Hippo asked his animal customers.

"Yes!" they all moaned or groaned or honked or sounded in whatever yes-sounds were appropriate to their species.

"Then come close to the fence and you give *them* a good show. Hedy, you shake it. And you, Lola, give your kid a breast-feeding. And how about a little sex from you, Mosie and Josie? And who volunteers to put on a fight?"

And as everyone knows, animals are actors at heart. When the safari came, the animals put on a good show. "Oh, if we people could only learn to be so natural," one member of the safari was heard to say. And another: "If you don't hurt them, they won't hurt you." The people got close to the fence. They didn't want to miss anything. They seemed quite pleased. "You couldn't see better at Barnum." "It was worth every banana," said a cosmopolite.

Hippo was ready for the zinger. "Get ready for the people performance, wild ones," he grunted. "Now step away from the fence." The animals moved back.

Zing! He shot some current through the fence. And the people gave the animals the performance they were promised.

"*Eeeeee,*" the ladies screeched.

"*Ouch,*" yowled the men.

Some threw their arms up. Some ran around in circles. One lady yelled, "I'm dying." "Even the city is safer than this," said an old man.

Hippo had given the people a good show and he had given the animals a good show, too. And he was in the bananas. He bought a purple satin robe trimmed with ermine tails, and a gold crown, and rode around the jungle in an open chariot.

"He's a king," said the camel.

"A king," the zebra said.

"A king among beasts," said the rhinoceros.

"He's a hippopotamus who rolls in the mud," said the open-bill stork. "Every animal knows the lion is king of the jungle."

"And they know that you ride on Hippo's back and eat the snails that ride along, too," said the zebra. "Hippo's a king. He's king enough for me."

47

And Hippo feels like a king. And that's king enough for him.

## MORAL

**He who can earn enough bananas in the jungle can be considered a king.**

# RISK

The Loon stops at Wally's Watering Hole to unwind. Old birds and young, male animals and female, stop at Wally's after a day's work. Lions drink there with lambs. There is a cacophony of roars and laughter, yakking and squawking.

"My father is for the birds," wails The Loon.

And a lion next to him yowls, "What a beast of a day I've had. I had a run-in with a tiger. He scared the hell out of me. Hey, what's eating you, Loon?"

"I told you. It's my father. I'll bet you never came across a dog like him. He knows I care for my mother like a son, and he tells me about all his conquests with his chippies. He doesn't give a second thought to how I feel."

The Loon, seeing that he has all of The Lion's attention, continues his complaints:

"I work for the old diver. He has me pattering about all the time and he hardly ever lets me use my wings. Let me give you an example: Today a buyer came to our showroom. I was ready to clinch a big sale when in walks my father with his order pad. He takes the order and then calls me a loon for not being able to write up any decent

49

orders. Get it? He writes up *my* order. And he's a real nuthead. You can't tell from one minute to the next how he is going to act. I hate the old loon.''

"Hold it, Junior," says The Lion. "Why don't you go to your dad and tell him that out of respect of your mother you don't want to hear about his carryings-on any more. And ask him if he would leave you to your own resources when you are trying to put over a deal. Knowing dads, I think he would respect you more if you ask this of him.''

"You don't know my father. He's a loony bird. He'll never go along with this straight talk.''

"Then tell him 'or else.'"

The Loon says it sounds like a good idea. He will try it. He and The Lion exchange 'see ya laters' and each goes on his way.

The next evening they meet again at Wally's, greeting each other like old friends. "How's your dad," asked The Lion.

"He should drop," says The Loon.

"So you talked to him. What did he say?"

"I couldn't talk.''

"Why? You seem able to talk. You're talking to me now. What's stoppping you?''

"It's the 'or else.'"

"There's no other way. You have to say 'or else.' I wouldn't be a lion today if I didn't learn to say 'or else.' Why didn't you say it?''

"Well . . . ," says The Loon.

"Well, what?''

"Well, when I thought of saying 'or else' I realized it can lead to 'I'll leave.' And then I remembered there's a special something between me and my dear daddy that I wouldn't like to ever lose.''

# RISK

And he pulled out his Visa charge card, pays his check, and flies off in his private jet to his cushioned nest.

## MORAL

**If you're not prepared to take the risk, then all you can do is keep squawking.**

# HOW TO CATCH A
# SPARROW

A nest for rent indicates a bird's intention to change his space, to fly off to better climes, to build a new nest with a mate. Whatever Harriet's specific intent, her advertisement in *The Bird Whistle* brought her a fine response.

Harriet was a sparrow. Her mate had flown off with a chippie. No tremendous loss to her, but her appetite for the male still stirred within her. How could she find a male to cozy up with on cold nights? She would look for a sparrow, a sparrow shy and forlorn, and set her sights for him. She targeted in on Harold.

Harold was a big bird in his chosen field, but in the field of love, as Harriet had suspected, he was indeed as shy, forlorn, and lonely as any bird could be. He bemoaned his fate. Oh, why did his beloved have to fly to the Great Beyond? She was the only female who would ever understand him. She didn't mind that he was the drab, colorless creature he knew himself to be. She had been devoted to him as no other bird could ever be. No bird could take her place.

Harriet knew that she would have to work hard to win Harold, but that didn't frighten her away. For a sparrow, life is never a song. She would study him, try to please him. She would woo him and win.

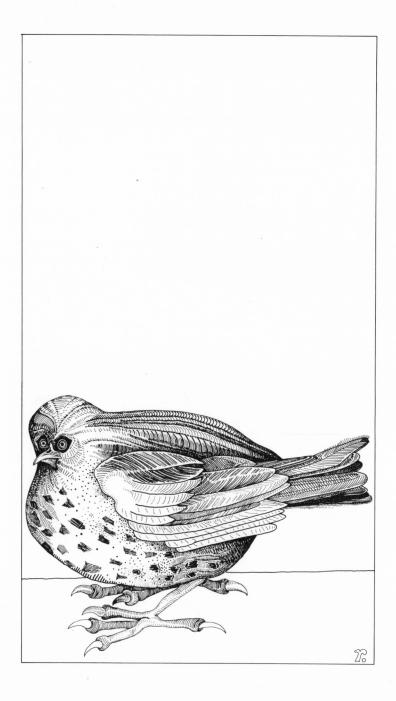

## HOW TO CATCH A SPARROW

Harriet stopped at the birdbath where Harold was known to drink. She told him she had known his mate.

"She was an angel. A saint," he moaned.

"She had wings," Harriet peeped sympathetically. And thus her pursuit began.

He said he liked Bach. She said she liked Bach.

He sneezed. She brought him some bird's nest soup.

He fluffed his tail. "You're the sexiest bird I've ever known," she chirped.

She felt she was making progress.

"I like you, Harriet," he said, "but I am unworldly."

"I know," she said. "I like unworldly birds." (He was getting ready to propose).

"And my mate knew I was unworldly and she told me so."

"She was wise to tell you so." (She would line their nest with polka-dot silk.)

"She said I would be a pushover for any tricky chippie."

"How lucky that a tricky chippie never got her wings on you." (What was he leading up to?)

"And she made me promise that after she passed on, I wouldn't be hasty about taking another mate. So I don't plan to wed for a long, long, long, long time."

And she had thought she was making progress! Poor Harriet! Her very being itched for a mate. How long can any little bird wait! She had tried as hard as any little sparrow could to win Harold. She would not give up now. She had tried every trick. But why not try an old trick in a new way? But which old trick? Which new way? She stared at her branch of her old maple for inspiration. How she loved her nest on her branch of her old maple! But she would give it up gladly to move in with a male, to move in with Harold, her beloved. Oh, inspiration. She needed inspiration. And happily, her branch gave her the inspiration she sought. An old trick, yes, used in a new way, a way that would use the help of some birds who had current needs, needs that she could fill.

"Nest for rent," she advertised. "High-rise Maple. View of the sky. Down-to-earth rental. Furnished with finest wool hairs and feathers. Only first five male applicants will be considered. Perch on Limb #16 Monday at 8 P.M. and wait for Harriet."

"I must say 'adieu,' Harold," she said when she met Harold on Monday. "I will have to wed another."

"Which other?" he asked.

"Which other?" she said. "I'm not sure, but I'll choose one. They're all lined up waiting, waiting for me. Would you like to see?"

She took Harold to her home nest. And there, as she had hoped, perched on Limb #16 were five sparrows.

"Who are you waiting for?"

"Harriet! Harriet! We're all waiting for Harriet," they chirped in chorus.

Harold shivered with fear that one of the five sparrows would wisk Harriet away. "Will you be mine? Now. Quick. Please," he asked.

And Harriet caught her sparrow.

---

**MORAL**

**Current shortages can fill some bird's needs.**

---

# PRODIGAL SON

His handmaidens were getting old and set in their ways. They insisted on service plates under his guinea hen and they wouldn't allow him to wear his napkin around his neck. "Why not a game of footsie with a dragonette at Esalen?" thought Benny.

"Don't take any wooden nickels," he told Trusty. He felt he didn't have to give Trusty any further instructions. Trusty knew how to get things done. Trusty was suspicious enough to catch any spy who might be lurking about. He could be deadly to an enemy but protective of Benny; he was a snake Benny felt he could trust. Benny was careful not to give Trusty enough bread to make him dangerous to him, but Benny gave Trusty enough perks so that Trusty would be contented.

"Have dinner on me, any night you want," he said, "and remember, guard the formula with your life."

"May I never live to crawl on my belly if I let any creature know the secret."

Benny was a dragon in the power business. He had developed a formula that when added to his own flames

gave them such force that they could move mountains. His formula produced for him great wealth.

Benny knew he was envied, that there was hardly a creature in the animal kingdom who would not like to be in his place. He knew that many a creature in the animal kingdom was conniving to become a dragon himself. He had to be eternally vigilant. But he had to trust at least one creature so he could keep production moving. And he had to have a little fun, too.

Trusty prepared the formula. He felt powerful. He felt as powerful as a dragon. "Why can't I become a dragon?" he thought. "I have scales like a dragon. I have a fire burning inside me. And I have the formula. All I need is enough bread and I can become a dragon, too, like Benny." So. . . .

"I love you, Wilma," he said. "Will you marry me, oh ravishing one?" Wilma was a rich little worm.

"Yes, yes, yes," she said.

Wilma wiggled to Trusty's hiss. One day, when Trusty hissed, Wilma didn't wiggle quickly enough. Trusty hissed fire and brimstone. He frightened poor Wilma into the willies and she willied herself into Kingdom Come. And she willed Trusty lots of bread, enough bread to go into his own business, which he did—using, of course, Benny's secret formula.

When Benny returned from his vacation, he found he had a competitor. "That snake in the grass!" he said. He had to stop this creature who spoke out of both sides of his mouth—out of one with loyalty and out of the other with treachery. He sued Trusty, which was his right, and he lost his suit, which was a vagary of the judicial process.

Unhappily, Benny watched Trusty's business prosper. Yet happily, his own business prospered, too. There seemed to be room in the market place for both of them.

With more power available to all creatures, new customers found need for additional power.

Benny watched Trusty gradually turn into a dragon, with the rewards, the responsibilities, and the threats to survival of being a dragon. He hated Trusty, but at the same time respected him. Dragons respect each other. That is the way of dragons.

Benny now handled his business with consummate care. Now he entrusted a leopard with his formula (a leopard could not change his spots). He looked under each blade of grass himself for snakes. He battened down the hatches each night and buried the bottom line. He knew that tomorrow the unexpected would happen. And he tried to be prepared.

Seven years and a day later, Trusty called on Benny.

"We're both dragons now, Benny. I want to thank you for all you taught me. Because of your good training, I'm a dragon today. And I understand your problems and you understand mine. You don't hurt me. I don't hurt you. But, unfortunately, we both have a common enemy . . ." And he told Benny about a poisonous snake who had their formula and was going into competition with them. "Let's both sue him and he'll never be able to make it."

For a fleeting moment Benny enjoyed the irony of the situation. Trusty, the snake who had stolen his formula, was coming to him for help. But rightly so. They had a common foe. Who knew what could happen with more competition! The market might become saturated with the product of this new competitor and Benny might be flooded out. This interloper could conceivably become the cause of Benny's demise. Maybe he should sue. "Who is this snake?" he asked.

"Mmm—I don't know," said Trusty. "I hear he's a foreigner from the south. For all I know, he could even be a foreign agent. I sent spies to find out who he is and they found nobody at the address he's supposed to be working from. A snake like that I never came across. We have to sue, Benny. It's our right and our duty."

Benny said he would think about it. He would let Trusty know his decision shortly. "And we'll let bygones be bygones. How's the family?"

Trusty left and awaited Benny's reply.

Benny went about his business and wondered what action he should take against the new menace. Ah, life was never free of problems. Just when he was beginning to feel secure again, why did he have to have this complication? And, if he should want to sue, where could he find this new enemy, this cobra, this serpent who had designs of becoming a dragon himself?

Benny did not have to think too long or too hard. "I am Serpent X of Company of the South, Limited," hissed a snake through some blades of grass. "Meet me tonight at the 79th Street Pier and bring five Cuban cigars with you. We'll talk business, eh?"

Benny went there that evening. He saw a snake crawling slowly towards him.

"Serpent X?" he asked.

The snake hissed in assent.

"Of Company of the South, Limited?" he asked.

The snake hissed again. "Do you have my cigars?" he asked.

Benny felt uneasy. There was something rotten here. Maybe he should never trust a snake. Or maybe it was just his suspicious nature. A dragon had to be suspicious at all times. But at dusk, this snake looked just like a snake he knew. Maybe all snakes looked alike at dusk. Benny would ask him. "Do you happen to know a snake from the We Steal 'Em and Double-Deal 'Em Energy Company called Trusty?"

"My cigar?"

Benny handed him a cigar.

"How perceptive you are. That snake is my brother."

"You can't be Trusty's brother," said Benny. "Trusty told me with his own mouth that his brother lives around the corner in Snake Alley and you're from the south."

"South, shmouth," said the snake. "I live around the corner. An imposter doesn't have to tell the truth. I let word get around that I am from the south because I can't let Trusty know who his competition is. Now, if you promise not to tell Trusty any of this, we can get down to business."

Benny was silent for a few minutes. He wanted the significance of what he had just heard to sink in. "If Trusty is your brother, then you are turning on your own brother."

"Yes, I am turning on my own brother. And why shouldn't I? Trusty talked me into giving up my own business to work for him six months ago. I did, even though I should have known better—since we were little rattlers I always got the dirty end of things when I had anything to do with Trusty. When he became afraid I would know too much, he threw me out. What was I to do? I had little ones to feed and no job. I'll ruin my snake of a brother if it's the last thing I do. And I don't care who I ruin with him."

"Ha," said Benny. "What can you do? You're a snake, a harmless snake. So you put your name on your own stock certificate! You know it doesn't mean a thing without the secret formula. And where can you get the bread? You've got a mouthful of cotton and you're hissing in the dark."

The snake spoke slowly and deliberately. "I have power. I have the formula. I can get the bread."

Benny had to put this viper in his place. He would not let himself be intimidated. He would not let this insidious one muscle in on his territory. He snorted thunder and lightning. He snorted out a double blast of fire. That would let Frusty know who had the real power.

"Do you know what $3$ u f o x $2$ m.f.h. to the nth degree means?" asked the snake.

Benny did not have to answer this question. He knew his own formula only too well. So there were three who knew it now! But what ordinary snake could get the bread? "Ha! where do you expect to get the bread from?" he asked.

"You seem to forget," said Frusty, "that I am a frustrated snake. And frustrated snakes with enough hate can activate their venom. I would do anything to destroy Trusty, and, if I have to destroy you in order to destroy him, I would do that gladly. We can all go down together. Now you know I have the formula. And you know it is the correct formula. If you won't take me under your wing, I will publish the formula in the trade journals. Any creature who wants to will then be able to make it. And you will go *pfft.*" Frusty blew cigar smoke into Benny's face to emphasize the point.

So this was a shakedown. Benny took a deep puff on his cigar. He tried to keep cool. He was a dragon. No snake could get him to crawl on his belly. "What do you want from me?" he asked.

"A family," Frusty said sweetly. "You see, my father was a stingy snake. He had lots of bread but he wouldn't give me a morsel. And you know my brother is a low-down, no-good snake. So what kind of family do I have? You, Benny, have a reputation for being beneficent. Benny the Beneficent, they call you. Would you be my daddy? Would you be my daddy and give me all the bread I need to keep my business going? What do you say? And remember, not a word of this to my brother."

A shakedown if Benny had ever heard one. "I make no promises. I'll let you know," said the dragon. Frusty crawled away.

Benny thought long and hard. True, Frusty would be better as a son, albeit a prodigal one. But Frusty was still a snake. It would be better for Benny, he reasoned, to align himself with a dragon. Trusty had already proven himself. He had been able to fight off enemies in the past and he would be able to do it again. He was a winner. Benny respected him even though he hated him—dragons respect each other. When threatened, he knew that for survival dragons had to stand together.

But there was more than one way to kill a snake. Why did he have to enter the battle at all? He could set the stage and it would be inevitable that the two brothers would fight. Let them destroy each other. Or, if one only were to fall in battle, he would be no worse off than he was now.

What about the formula? Would Frusty publish it in the trade journals as he had threatened? Benny was a dragon—he expected eternal change. When tomorrow came, he would tackle it. He had superior strength.

He went to see Trusty. "I know who the enemy is," he said, and he snorted. "And you know who the enemy is," he said, and he snorted the appropriate amount of fire. And he told Trusty who the enemy was.

And he leaned back and waited for the explosion.

---

### MORAL

**Believe me, it's not easy to be a dragon.**

---

# THE CHICKEN COOP

Leon was a rooster who found himself in the chicken coop one day. He didn't choose to go into the coop. He chose to take a mate and a necessary accompaniment to taking a mate was taking up residence in the coop. His buddies had chosen the coop months before and they had little chickies to play with and to perpetuate their breed. He had held off long enough. So, what the hell.

He asked the chicken he thought had the best genes, the chicken he thought could make life a little easy for him, to be his bride. So they invited a few friends for drinks, had some corn and some chicken feed, and Leon and Lisa were married. And they moved into their own coop. And there was Leon, all cooped up. "How did I get into this?" he cried. "I was a bird who used to rule the roost. I can't stand being cooped up. I need space."

Leon couldn't stand the chicken coop, but he was there nonetheless. Every morning, every single morning, he had to cock-a-doodle-doo, cock-a-doodle-doo, cock-a-doodle-doo to wake up Lisa so that she'd go out and scratch for feed. And every day the coop seemed to close in more on him.

Through the wires he watched the young chicks undulate their tail feathers. He would chase them when he could, but he always had to go back to his coop. When he didn't chase the chicks, he spaced out so he wouldn't have to look at the chicken wire that held him captive.

True, he could have run away, but a chicken is chicken. He doesn't run too far from home and he won't run without good reason.

One June morning: "When you amble about today, dear," said Lisa, "will you buy me an alarm clock? I hate to think that you have to get up so early just to cock-a-doodle-doo me awake."

Leon was so excited he felt he could fly. Lisa had just presented him with the reason he was looking for, the reason that would buy him back his reason. "You want ME to pay for an alarm clock for YOU? Don't give me any of that shit! I'm up to your tricks. You're trying to do me out of the chicken feed I've socked away."

Lisa was bewildered.

"Don't worry," screeched Leon, "I didn't get it from your scratchings. I had to sell my food stamps for it."

"You don't understand, Leon. I'm perfectly willing to pay for the alarm clock. And if you don't want me to have one, I don't have to buy it at all."

"Besides, you're a big fat hen. And just because you lived like a princess with your mother, that's no excuse not to clean the coop while you're out scratching. And you don't wear your feathers like a sexy chick and you're a nag, nag, nag, and you don't give me enough space."

And he flew the coop.

## MORAL

If you want to get out of the coop, you can always find a reason.

# THE GOPHER

George was a gopher. If he had only had a father to support him while he was growing up, he could have been a success and had his own gopher to order around, but since he wasn't a success and wanted to taste the finer things in life, he took a job with Bernard. At least with this job he wouldn't have to live in a hole and subsist on potatoes, and he could share some of the goodies.

"Will you run down to the deli and get me a corned beef on rye with mustard, hold the pickle," said Bernard. This bear's success was no accident. He worked hard and was satisfied with no less than perfection. Since he had no time to fetch the meals he could afford, he hired George to fetch them for him.

"Will do," squeaked George, wearing the hangdog look of his breed, and he scurried off.

He gave the waiter at the deli his order. When served, he put a sandwich in each pouch—one for him and the other for Bernard—and ambled back, holding the pickle in his mouth.

"Where's the mustard?" roared Bernard. "Even a baboon would know that a corned beef sandwich should come with mustard! And who told you to bring a pickle?

Don't you check anything? What were you doing when the waiter prepared the order? Sleeping?"

The bear and the gopher ate their lunch together in silence. Bernard couldn't enjoy the sandwich without the mustard and George couldn't enjoy it either, because of Bernard's complaint about his not delivering the mustard. He had brought the meat and the bread. Why couldn't Bernard appreciate him for what he did right?

But that was the way things were. And since he wanted to taste the finer things in life, he would have to run these errands and run the risk of making Bernard angry. Tomorrow was another day and he would try to do better tomorrow.

"Will you run to the Chinese take-out and bring me an order of pork chow mein?" asked Bernard the next day.

George had no good thoughts on getting the chow mein.

It took a lot of effort for him to go for the chow mein. It took effort for him to talk to the waiter. It took effort for him to explain to the waiter exactly what he wanted. And to face Bernard on his return and find out what he had done wrong was the most painful matter of all. If he had been a hermit with no sophisticated tastes, his life would have been easier. Only the thought of eating some chow mein kept him going.

He ordered the chow mein. The waiter served him his order. This time he would check it carefully. He took it apart.

Two chow meins? Two chow meins.

Two mustards? Two mustards.

Two pigeon bloods? Two pigeon bloods.

And what was this? Fortune cookies? He didn't order them. He'd better not take them. Well, he could eat them on the way.

## THE GOPHER

George was satisfied that he had accomplished his mission to perfection. He felt Bernard couldn't possibly find fault today. George presented the feast to Bernard.

Bernard took the package apart. George could see by the way the big bear's body blew up that he had goofed again. "No noodles?" roared Bernard. "Any monkey knows you can't eat chow mein without noodles! Where was your head?"

George's head hung so low that he looked more like a ball waiting to be kicked than a gopher. He didn't want to goof. On occasion he didn't goof. He would see that he never goofed again.

George dug a hole. Then he dug a series of corridors. And at the farthest end of the longest corridor, he built a nest. And he lay down in his nest with his forelegs close to his sides. He kept his mouth clamped shut. And he vowed to stay that way forever so he could never make a mistake again.

### MORAL

**You'll never make a mistake if you don't get out of bed.**

# SULTRY SQUIRREL

Sultry Squirrel went down the river to seek her fortune. "I want to gather lots of nuts," she said. She got a job with Dry-'Em-Don't-Fry-'Em Nut Company.

"Hm," said Solly-Boss Squirrel when he saw Sultry's bushy tail.

"Hm," said Sultry Squirrel when she got a hundred-fifty nuts at the end of the week for keeping the work records. Then, "Peanuts!" when she found she could eat up the nuts in three days.

She would like to have a fortune like Solly-Boss. "How did you make your fortune?" she asked him.

"With hard work and capital," he said proudly, puffing out his chest.

Hard work was easy for Sultry. But capital . . . she would have to work on that.

"You work too hard, Solly-Boss," she said as she fluttered her tail seductively. "You need some fun. Let's do nutty things together."

They did nutty things together and they had lots of fun. "I'm having lots of fun," said Solly-Boss.

"You're so je ne sais quoi," said Sultry. And Solly-Boss thought she was so adorable that he gave her bags

and bags of nuts. And they did more nutty things. And they had lots more fun together.

"Oooooh, you're sweet," said Sultry.

"You're sweet, too, sweet as a cashew," he said. And he gave her more and more bags of nuts.

Did Sultry squirrel some nuts away? And buy a mink like a classy dame? Mm, yes. And she strung some nuts into chains and used them for drapes; she made some into elephants and formed some to make apes; she made some into dollies and turned some into dolls' dishes: she made horses and bosses and fish bowls and fishes.

"How artistic," said Solly-Boss. "But no more nuts."

"No nuts, no Sultry," she declared.

And she locked her door and she moved away.

One day Solly-Boss went for a walk near the river and he saw a new shop with a big neon sign: SULTRY'S NUTTY NICETIES. He peeked in the windows and saw shelves and shelves, and counters and aisles, filled with Sultry's artistic creations—all for sale.

"That rodent!" said Solly-Boss.

Capital!

**MORAL**

**Don't give nuts to a squirrel if you can't take the loss.**

# THE FISH WHO
# COULDN'T SAY "NO"

Mackeral nibbled with White Fish. She nibbled with Blue. She nibbled with Snapper. She nibbled with Carp. Not to mention Codfish and Scrod. She believed that lunching with her friends showed them she was *really* their friend. But the truth, which she was hardly aware of herself, was that she couldn't say "No."

She lunched with them whenever she was invited. And she seemed to have a lunch date every day of her life. Mackeral was content with the way she was living. She thought herself a good skate until, one day. . . .

"There's going to be a whale of a show at Mermaid's Hall tomorrow morning. Would you like to join me?" asked Blue.

"I'd love to," said Mackeral, even though she didn't give any thought as to whether or not she would like to see the show.

Later in the day she heard from White Fish. "My path will cross yours tomorrow. Would you like to lunch with me at noon?"

"I'd love to," she said. "But I'm going to a show with Blue tomorrow, and that usually means lunch afterwards." But she couldn't say "No" to White—"I'll tell her I have a previous engagement and I'll have lunch with you." Now White would know she was truly her friend.

"Do you expect me to have lunch with you tomorrow?" she asked Blue.

"Whatever you wish," said Blue. "I am a free-swimming fish. I can come and go as I please, and I can meet you or not as you please. Why do you ask? Do you have other plans after the show? What do *you* want to do?"

If Mackeral had answered the question honestly, she would have said, "I don't care as long as I straighten out this mess." She had gotten in touch with Blue to resolve the problem of the possibly conflicting lunch date. And with the opening Blue gave her she should have been able to tell Blue that she wouldn't meet her for lunch. Even a flounder would have been able to tell Blue that.

But face to face with Blue, Mackeral couldn't say that. In reconstructing the motives for her inept behavior later, she convinced herself she didn't want to hurt Blue's feelings by letting her know she had chosen another fish to lunch with (especially since the fish was Blue's sworn enemy), even though Blue didn't know she was lunching with White, and even though Blue had made it clear that it didn't matter to her what Mackeral did. So Mackeral said, "I want to have lunch with *you*." And with that declaration, she hoped that Blue understood that she was saying, "I am *your* friend."

Now, alas, she really had two lunch dates with two feuding fish at the same time. And it came about, she believed, because she was a truer friend than almost any fish swimming in the waters. She felt terrible. Oh, why must the *good* suffer so? What was she to do? She could go to the show with Blue and then leave her. She could say her grandmother died. That would be terrible. Or she could cancel her lunch date with White. And that would be terrible, too.

After splashing about all night thinking, she decided she would tell White that she would have lunch with her at three, and then she would be able to have lunch with both White Fish and Blue by having it at different times. It wouldn't be the best thing for her waistline, but what wouldn't she do for a friend.

So the next morning she told White she would meet her for lunch at three.

"Fine," said White.

Now wasn't that easy. Mackeral was relieved.

Unhappily, White had said 'Fine' because she didn't absorb immediately the significance of what Mackeral had said. But when the stench reached her. . . . So! Mackeral was pushing her aside for another fish! So after all the friendship she had offered Mackeral, Mackeral was treating her like any poor fish whose mate had gone to his watery grave! Her blood began to boil. "You! You! You stinking mackeral with your holier-than-thou ways," she blurped. "You're nothing but a cold-blooded, rotten fish. Shall I tell you what they call you in the currents? The truth? A go-between. A pimp. A no-good slimy pimp. One day you'll get yours like the common fish you are. If you want to know when I'll meet you again, the answer is 'Never.' I happen to have plans at three and for the rest of my life."

Mackeral was shaken. So that's what sweet White Fish thought of her. And she had thought that she was pleasing White Fish by sharing her company with her. "I must have really been 'out to lunch' when I said 'yes' every day,'' she told herself. What was it that Bluefish had asked her? 'What do *you* want to do?' Now she knew: LEARN TO SAY 'NO.'

She has actually said it on occasion and no fish seems to have noticed the difference.

### MORAL

**You don't get into any more trouble doing what you want to do than doing what you think others want you to do.**

# GOOD WORK

Once upon a time, not too long ago, there was a mama bear, a baby bear, and a big sister bear. There were three brother bears and a papa bear in this bear family, too. But we are not concerned with them in this story because they were out hunting and fishing most of the time; Papa was teaching his young sons how to hunt and fish and provide food for themselves and their female kin. We are concerned here only with home and hearth, with Mama and her female cubs, and with Mama's teaching her female cubs how to clean house and prepare the food for their male kin.

It was spring-cleaning time. Big Sister was collapsing from tiredness. She had just finished scrubbing the walls, beating the carpets, ironing the bed linens, polishing the pots, and making fish stew for dinner. Big Sister hadn't volunteered to do this work; Mama had asked her to do it. "Someday you will have a family and a den of your own," she had said, "and it is my duty to see that you learn to do the housework."

Big Sister didn't mind doing the work when she thought about how hard Mama was working herself, and when she thought she would like to make life easier for Mama if she could. And she didn't mind it when she thought about the den she would have for herself, and about having her own family someday. She would want to do a good job then and it would be a good idea for her to practice now. But she did mind doing so much work when she thought about Baby Bear, and when she thought about the fact that her three brothers had been born after baby was born, so that Baby wasn't such a baby any more. And why did Baby have the simple task of dusting the pedestal of the dining table and the legs of the dining chairs only? And why did Mama say that Baby was the best duster she ever knew?

Of course, Mama said Big Sister did an excellent job, and Big Sister knew she did, but why did she get all the hard work, the dirty work? There must be a reason.

Big Sister tried to think of what that reason could possibly be. As she thought, she got more and more angry. She was so angry that she took little bites up and down the length of her left foreleg. Mama called the doctor when she saw all the lumps, and the doctor said it was the strangest disease he had ever seen—in all the diseases he knew that manifested themselves in lumps, the lumps always appeared on all four limbs. Mama gave Big Sister porridge and toast in bed, and Big Sister liked that. But the lumps went down in two days and Big Sister was put back on heavy work.

"Why?" Big Sister asked herself time and time again. "Why do I get the dirty work?" One day, while she was ironing the Christmas tablecloth, she heard Baby ask Mama if she wanted her to dust the seats of the chairs, since sometimes when she dusted the legs the cloth accidentally touched the seat.

"You'll have enough to do, Baby, when you take a mate and have your own den to take care of. You're only a little cub. Why don't you run along and play?"

"How can Mama be so unfair?" thought Big Sister. "Maybe Mama is the mean stepmother, like the stepmother in 'Cinderella.' That's it. That's why Mama reads 'Cinderella' to us every night. She doesn't want to come right out and tell me I'm her stepcub. Reading the story

is her way of telling me that I'm not her natural-born cub. But Mama's not mean. Mama's nice and she works so hard herself and I'd help her more willingly if she weren't so partial to Baby . . ."

Hsssssssss. Big Sister heard a hiss and she smelled something burning. Oh, tragedy of tragedies! While ironing, she had burned a hole right in the middle of the Christmas tablecloth.

"Mama, Mama, Mama! I'm so sorry! I'll be more careful! I'll never burn anything again ever in my whole life," she cried.

"That's all right, dear," said Mama Bear. "These things happen once in a while."

And Big Sister was as careful as she could be.

But the next week, as she was polishing the big brass teapot, she was thinking that the wolf who hung around their door was really her real mother. Mama always said she wanted to keep the wolf away from their door and that was probably because when Big Sister was born to the wolf, the wolf couldn't find enough for her to eat and had carried her to Mama Bear, who took her in. Mama would have taken in a starving creature because Mama was kind, but nature forced Mama to be kinder to her natural cub than to the foundling that Big Sister was. And Mama wanted to keep her despite her lesser love for Big Sister, and Mama didn't want her to know these facts, and that's why she didn't want the wolf around so the wolf wouldn't tell her. And with this thought—CRASH— Big Sister dropped the kettle right on Mama's favorite cut-glass platter, and broke it to smithereens.

"I'm sorry, Mama. I'm so, so sorry. I don't know how I could have done such a careless thing," she cried.

"You couldn't help it, dear, I'm sure. These things happen once in a while," said Mama.

"What do you want me to clean next, Mama? I'll do anything to make up for this loss."

# GOOD WORK

Mama looked at Big Sister with a strange look, then closed her eyes as if she were deep in thought, sighed, and said, "You'll have enough to do when you take a mate, Big Sister, and have your own den and cubs to take care of. You're only a little cub yourself. Why don't you run along and play?"

Oh, happy day! So Mama wasn't the mean step-mother Big Sister thought she was. And Big Sister wasn't Cinderella or the wolf's whelp after all. At long last Mama was treating her the same as she was treating Baby Bear. She *would* run along and play. But first she would ask Baby if she would like to play with her.

She crept under the table. "When you finish your work, Baby, would you like . . ." And Big sister took a close look at the pedestal. It had heavy wax buildup, pawprints and watermarks, kickmarks, smudges, streaks, and a good deal of soil. Big Sister was shocked. Maybe Baby was a bigger baby than she had thought she was. "I'll help you do a good job, Baby," she said, "and then will you come out and play with me?"

Baby roared with laughter. "Do you think I'm stupid or something?" she said. "Let's look at it this way: If I do a good job, then I'll have to cook and clean and scrub just like you. And I don't think I'd like that at all."

---

### MORAL

**Beware: The reward for doing a good job is more work.**

---

# CAT'S CLAWS

Once there was a cat and his name was Alley. He was an alley cat. He had claws like a tiger and he scratched for his grub. He was so good at scratching that he was invited to join Hubba Bubba's Natural Grub Company. He started at the ground and he scratched his way up to top management.

Life for Alley was not all business. He loved Felina. She was the cat's meow. He took her for his bride. "I'll bring in grub enough for both of us," he said. "You just look pretty and lick my coat and roll around in the sunshine and let me admire your beautiful belly." Felina took the vows and she was a good mate. She was easy-going, faithful, and home-loving. She was a lovely looking cat, but she lost her claws.

Now don't be alarmed; it has happened before and it will happen again. Many a cat finds that when she lets her tom scratch for her grub, her claws disappear. Felina didn't mind. In fact, she rather liked it. She learned to get what she wanted without scratching for it. She went to the Wednesday afternoon Gossip Club. She whammed a

few golf balls around on Tuesdays and Fridays. In her time and place it was the thing to do.

Alley was proud. And he was a fighter. He killed rats and mice and helped build Hubba Bubba into one of the biggest prepared cat-food companies in the business. A sharp cat.

But time took its toll. And places must be left for the younger cats. And alley cats don't have much of a place in today's market in any case, what with all the prestigious schools of business administration and all the new business machines.

"May we present you with this gold watch and the address of the nearest pensioners' office," said Smartface, cum laude graduate of Catwalk University. And he gave Alley the sack. And now Alley lost his claws.

He became timid. He had a hangdog look. He didn't know how to spend his days. Perhaps Felina could teach him. She had been without claws for many a year.

"I'd like to go to the supermarket with you, Felina," he said. He had worked in market research. This might be interesting for him.

"Fiddlesticks," she said. "I'm perfectly capable of wheeling the shopping cart around myself."

"Then how about your Gossip Club? I'd like to go there and hear some of the catty ones." Alley had experience at business cats' luncheons. He could make a comparative study.

"We couldn't talk with you around. What do you think we talk about anyway?"

Alley went to the Howlers' Pub where the toms stopped for a beer after work. His old pals no longer responded to his howls. "Why don't you go to Marbella and lie in the sun?" they asked.

# CAT'S CLAWS

Alley saw there was no place for him in his factory town. He did what he felt he had to do. He took his mate to Marbella's sunny shores, where hardly a cat who has claws lives.

"There's no place like Marbella," he says as he sifts the sands through his paws. "This is the life."

## MORAL

**Many a cat without claws lives like a dog.**

# THE KID

High on a cliff, almost touching the sky, lived a mountain goat family. There was Mother Goat, Godfrey Goat, and The Kid.

Now Godfrey Goat was not The Kid's father; The Kid's father had left Mother when The Kid was just an embryo. Godfrey was Mother's new mate and Mother felt she was lucky to have him for a mate. He was willing to live with her even though she had The Kid to raise. He was willing to stay with her past the rutting season. And he brought in good pickings.

Mother tried to give Godfrey a quiet and peaceful home. It was easy for her to do so when The Kid was off playing with the other kids. It was not so easy for her to do so when The Kid was close to home.

He was a frisky little chap, and quite boisterous. He would slide down the mountain near their home and shriek like the devil. He was so noisy when he bounced down the rocks and did his stunts that even the eagles swooped down to see what all the noise was about.

# THE KID

Mother had to make The Kid understand that kids should be seen and not heard, especially when they were cliff-dwellers (think of the neighbors), and especially when there was a stepdaddy around.

One afternoon when The Kid was very noisy, Mother nudged him behind a snowpile. "Who the HELL do you think you are!" she hissed through her clenched teeth.

To The Kid, these words, especially the word "hell" from his ordinarily sedate mother, made him feel as if an avalanche had fallen on him. He couldn't understand why his mother was angry with him. All he was doing was having a good time.

Many times, as The Kid was growing up, his mother took him behind a rock, or a crag, or a snowpile, and she would hiss the question, "Who the HELL do you think you are!" The Kid didn't know the answer and he wasn't pleased with the question. One thing he was sure of was that it meant his mother didn't think much of him.

The Kid often played King of The Mountain with his friends and when he grew up he became king of the mountain, for he became the dominant male of the herd. Yet he never *felt* like king of the mountain. He felt more like a schmuck. And the question 'Who the HELL do you think you are!' plagued him. His mother no longer hissed it at him, but now he hissed it at himself.

One bitter, cold night, when he was making his plans to lead the herd to a neighboring mountain where they could find more vegetation, "Who the HELL do you think you are!" echoed in his head. This time it got his goat. He would answer:

"I'm not a sheep like Selwyn who balks at crossing gaps. . . . I'm not a grizzly who would do another goat harm. I am. . . . Who am I? Let me see. . . .

# THE KID

"I am Billy the Kid.

"I'm a devil who cares.

"I'm a high-mountain climber.

"I send grizzlies on the run.

"I am a watchdog. A lover.

"A barrel of laughs.

"I am Billy the Great, and that's great."

And he felt great. "Maybe," he mused, "maybe all my hell-raising helped me grow into the fearless mountain goat I am today . . ."

One thought led to another and his thoughts led to his mother. Why, he wondered, why did his mother try to make him believe he was a no-good kid? Now he pictured her with his mind's eye for the goat that she was—she with the upraised tail, ears flat against her head, her tongue nervously flicking in and out. Why, that was the posture of a scaredy-cat. Mother was scared. Scared of what, Mother? Scared that Godfrey would leave you? Scared that you would be left only with your cashmere to keep you warm? Scared to face the fact you didn't like the old goat and so let out your frustrations on me? Oh, Mother, I think you're chicken. It's not nice of you to make your kid your scapegoat.

"Who the HELL do you think you are?" He would give her his answer right now. No matter that it was four in the morning. No matter that Mother liked peace and quiet. He had waited long enough to give her his reply. He would not wait another minute

He went to her and nudged her shoulder with his big spiral horns. "Mother, I have the answer," he said.

"What answer?" she grumbled. "And who the HELL do you think you are, waking me up at this ungodly hour."

## THE KID

"I'll tell you, Mother, who the HELL I think I am. I think I am—one helluva great kid."

And indeed he was.

## MORAL

**Check it out, kids: You may be greater than you think.**

# IF IT LOOKS GOOD . . .

Deedee was a dear of a doe, but how was she to know? She was born under a star that was so busy reflecting in its own glory that it hardly shone on her at all. So Deedee felt she was not much and the bucks evidently agreed with her, for none sought her as his mate—which naturally confirmed Deedee's opinion of herself. "I am nothing if I do not have a mate," she told herself.

When she became so ashamed of being unwanted that she felt she couldn't face another deer, she went to the deepest part of the woods and hid. She hid so well that if her star had tried to find her it would have been unable to do so. Only Horace saw her, but he was blind to her presence. (Horace was a poet who stayed in the lonesome woods to meditate and to write his epic poem, "War and Peace in the Woods," without the disturbance of other deer.)

The hunting season came and with it the annual meeting of all the deer to plan their strategy. Should they all stay together or should they disband? Should they create new deer trails? Should the elderly and the sick stay on the outer rims of their herd or should they be protected in the inner circle? And what about the dogs—should they have practice runs to develop the stamina to outrun the dogs?

Every deer who wanted to survive knew he had to attend the meeting. Deedee knew that. But did she want to survive? Happy thought: If she didn't survive, she would no longer have to live with her great shame. A hunter's bullet, a dog, starvation might rescue her from her tragic fate.

"Mee, mee, mee," she heard. Where did this sound come from? She pushed through the brush. Oh, the darling! A little baby buck who had lost his mother. The poor little deer had no chance to survive. What might his life have become? She would comfort him as they both died together. She wept for little Apple—she gave him the name Apple for already he was the apple of her eye—and she wept for herself.

It was well for her to die, but why did this poor baby have to die? If she could find a deer who would act as his mother, perhaps he could survive. But who could take care of him? Horace? Surely not Horace. Why, Horace had not even looked up to see who was whimpering when Apple whimpered. And surely not her, for she was about to die.

Apple looked at her, his big black eyes filled with trust. She could not act as his mother. But she would have to. She would have to put aside her concerns about herself for the present. "Come on, Apple," she said, "we're going to a meeting."

She put some ferns over her eyes so she wouldn't see the looks of pity on the faces of the other deer when they saw she was still unmated. And she dragged Apple and herself to the meeting.

She heard the jovial sounds of the deer, the bravado before being hunted. There were Vicki, Caroline, Donna, and Lisa, all with mates. And there, too, was Horace stumbling along, moving up to the herd. Surprising that he was able to find his way there, thought Deedee. And there was Charlie. At one time she had thought that if he wanted her she would never accept him, and Charlie then mated with the most popular deer in the woods.

"I didn't know you had a little one, Deedee," said Charlie.

A little one? Charlie thought Apple was *her* little one. With the quick thinking of a deer who has to survive by wits, she said, "Yes, of course, my little one. And Horace, too. Horace! Horace! Come here, Horace! I'd like you to meet my friends," she said expansively.

"A little one and a mate, too," said Donna. "And you never told us. My, you keep secrets."

The deer shouted their congratulations and Horace, unaware of what their cheers were for, recited his epic poem of the deadliness of the hunter's gun.

And Deedee joined the pack with her head held high and her eyes on the lookout for the hunter's gun, like any proud deer who feels she is something.

### MORAL

**If you're concerned about how things look to others, looking good may be good enough.**

# THE WHOLE PIGEON

"'Bye, darling. Have a safe trip," said Pipi. Pipi was a warm-blooded bird with a relatively large brain, keen sight, a twenty-two-inch wing span, and a short, stout body covered with heavy brown plumage. Alexander was her mate. He had similar attributes except, of course, for the usual sexual differences. To most creatures they looked equal—equal in size, equal in attractiveness, equal in capability. Yet Alexander raced over high mountains, traveling across the grand oceans to the far corners of the world. And Pipi stayed in her pigeonhole and hardly fluttered her wings.

She was content to stay in her pigeonhole. She knew that as far or as wide as Alexander traveled, he always came home to her. And when he came home, he told her in his soft, cooing voice of his great adventures, of his conquests of space. And she listened, and felt she was well-traveled, too, for his life was her life. Alexander added to her life what she lacked in her own. He made her feel complete. He made her feel like a whole pigeon. "Tell me, tell me, tell me more," she would often coo to him. And he would pat her on the head and recall another detail and add it to his story.

Pipi took care of the home front. She chewed the grass and regurgitated it for her young. She enjoyed their delight in eating some of the fruits Alexander brought them. And she thought about how lucky she was to be able to enjoy the whole world through her mate.

But her fledglings grew up and flew away. Her nest

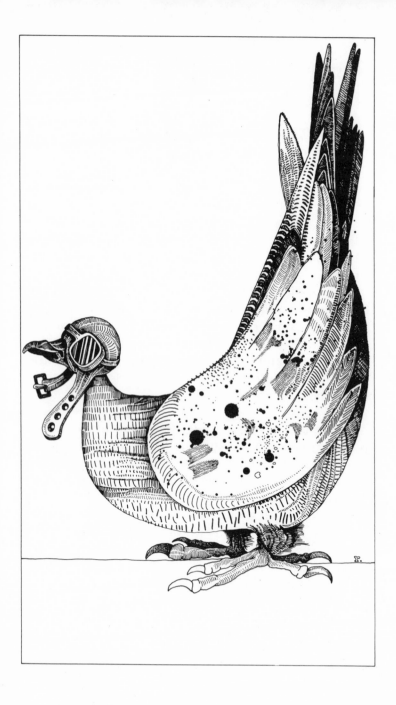

was empty. Time lay heavy on her wings. "I'd like to do something," she said to Alexander.

"What do you know?" he asked tenderly.

"Maybe I could learn something," she peeped. "Maybe I could learn to *do* something. Maybe I could learn—to fly high in the sky."

"You could never become a high flyer," he said. "You may have brown feathers like any fine pigeon, but you have a yellow streak."

Pipi knew she had it. She had often joked about it with Alexander. "I could never do that," she said to him when he told her of his great adventures. "I have a yellow streak."

She noticed how big it made him look when she told him she was yellow, and she liked him to look big, to seem head and neck above her. But, of course, that made her feel little—oh, so little—and she was afraid she was getting littler and littler, and that if she got much littler, Alexander might feel she was too little for him. But what could she do?

One day in early spring, Pipi went to the wildlife preserve to get some fresh seeds. She read the sign posted on a tree: "A 15-mile race will be held for The Most Unlikelies on the first day of summer. All novice fliers are urged to register here."

"What's it all about?" she asked a cat standing nearby.

"It's a race for birds who haven't used their wings much. Why don't you enter the pigeon race?"

"I hardly know how to use my wings at all," said Pipi. "I have a yellow streak. Besides, I don't want to rock my nest. And," she added proudly, "my mate does all my flying for me."

"Oh, one of those dependent birds. Many a bird lets her mate do all the flying. But do you know the glorious feeling of flying yourself? Your mate can't live your life for you, don't you know."

"And how do you know, wise cat?" said Pipi angrily. "What makes you an authority? You're not even a bird."

"So I'm a cat. But I'm a hep cat. Call me Hepzibah. We female felines have our problems, too. I'm learning how to go after what I want. You can learn how to do your own flying. It's all the same. Now do you, or don't you, want to learn?" said Hepzibah impatiently.

Pipi thought about it. Then she thought about Alexander—she always thought about Alexander. "I bet Alexander would be happy to see that I could carry my own weight. He'd be *so* happy to see that I could measure up. If I could fly long distances," she mused, "he'd *know* that I was a bird of worth." And she was happy at the thought of Alexander's happiness when he learned that she could fly. She pictured herself racing over high mountains, across the grand oceans to the far corners of the world, flying with her own two wings, flying just like Alexander did. Well, perhaps not as high, but flying high nonetheless.

"What a phenomenal idea!" said Pipi enthusiastically. "I don't know why I never thought about it before. I'll surprise Alexander. But how do I learn to fly high? Who can teach me?"

"Me," said Hepzibah. "You can learn the same way I learned to go after things. Learn the formula: Rate times time equals distance. Practice, practice, practice. Do some somersaults to distract the competition. And dovetail all your activities."

"I'll give it a fling," Pipi said casually. But she felt deep in her heart that she would do everything in her power to learn long-distance flying for in doing so, she felt, she would gain stature in Alexander's eyes.

Whenever Alexander went off on his long flights, Pipi went to the wildlife preserve. She practiced flying. She increased her rate and her time. Each time she flew, she flew higher and traveled a greater distance than she had flown on her previous flight. She flew farther and farther each day till she made the grade of Long Distance Flyer. She was ready—ready for the race.

On the first day of summer, she reported for the pigeon class for entrants. There were fruit pigeons and crowned pigeons, mourning doves and grey-ground doves, band-tails, red-bills, and quarrelsome carriers. "I'm going home," Pipi peeped under her breath. But having a yellow streak, she felt too yellow to even say it aloud, and she flew along with the other pigeons.

She flew in the race. She used strength she didn't know she had. She used her maximum wing power. She used all the skills she had mastered. She flew high, wide, and handsome. And she came in in second place. She was awarded second prize by the judges, a copper ankle bracelet.

Oh, how happy Alexander would be, she thought. She showed her prize to Alexander. Alexander did not seem happy. "A copper bracelet?" he said. "Phooey!"

Perhaps he didn't understand. She had a way, she knew, of not explaining things well. She would try to explain it to him more carefully. "It's for second place, darling," she said. "Aren't you proud of me? I can fly high and I even won the race. I believe it's quite an accomplishment for a bird as inexperienced as I am to win a race."

"A race for The Most Unlikelies?" Alexander laughed. "You entered such a foolish race? What bird would fly in a race like that anyway! No self-respecting pigeon, you can be sure. What made you enter that race?"

She reached up and gave him a peck on his cheek. "I wanted to surprise you. It was Hepzibah. She's a hep cat. She told me about the race and she taught me how to . . . go after what I want."

"You try to learn from a cat?" said Alexander. "You know that cats only stir up trouble. And what are you so excited about? You came in second. I wouldn't call that winning. And what proof do I have that you even came in in second place? You'll have to prove it to me." And with each angry word Alexander said, he tapped on Pipi's head.

But Pipi's head was swelled from the exhilaration she felt at the honor of coming in second, and when Alexander tapped her head, it hurt. "Take your foot off my head, Alexander," she said in a firm voice. "You're holding me down."

Alexander was unaccustomed to resistance from Pipi. No bird would give HIM orders. He flew into a rage. "Oh, so you're one of those, eh! You're too much for me!" he declared. And he flew away. "So he left, the cad!" she said.

Pipi waited for him to return. She was sure he would return soon and when he did return, he would understand that she flew just to please him. And he would regret the pain he had caused her. But he did not return.

Pipi knew she had to go on living. But how could she live without Alexander? Would she ever be able to coo or peep again?

Well, maybe she had better keep busy while she was waiting. Maybe she had better keep flying, now that she was a long-distance flyer. So she flew. She flew over high mountains. She flew across the grand oceans. She flew to faraway lands. It was good to fly. It was good to eat the exotic fruits and herbs she gathered herself. It was good to be able to gather enough to feed a whole brood.

Her yellow streak became fainter and fainter until it disappeared. And she felt much bigger now that she could fly on her own. But something was missing in her life. She didn't feel complete. She didn't feel like a whole pigeon.

"What should I do about the loneliness?" she asked Hepzibah.

"We're working on that," said the hep cat. "In time

101

we will know the answer. Would you rather Alexander got his jollies from putting you down?"

At that moment, if Pipi had decided to tell the truth she would have said, "Yes." But she said, "Perhaps. Perhaps servitude to a warm-bodied male is better than this lonely freedom. Do you have a line on which is the natural way?"

"Each to his own," said Hepzibah. "By-the-by, have you heard that Alexander is living in paradise with a lightweight chi-chi bird? It doesn't speak well for him that he would like that type of a bird."

"So that's what he wanted, the creep—a birdbrain of a pigeon. Well, he got just what he deserves. He can carry that helpless one around—with my blessings. I'd rather do my own flying anyway," she said. But like many a bird when hurt, Pipi's words did not reflect her true feelings. She felt abandoned. She felt desolate. What she would have done to be in this bird's paradise. Then her true feelings poured out with her little pigeon tears. "Why did I have to learn how to fly!" she wailed.

But, enough of this mourning! She would have to do something about her own life now. She would have to do something to assuage her loneliness.

She cooed a mating call high in the air. No high flier answered her call. "Coo, coo. Coo, coo, coo," she called. No response. "I must be cuckoo to send my love calls into the rarefied air. I don't need a high flier to take care of me any more. I can fly far and wide myself, but I need . . ."

One winter day, when she felt particularly lonely, she saw a male bird with ruffled feathers eating crumbs from the hand of a bird lady. She felt stirrings within her that couldn't be contained. She cooed her sexiest coo. "Hi, Ultimate One," she said, "why are you eating crumbs?"

"I'm weak-livered and I have a yellow streak. I only take what comes my way."

She could surely gather enough to feed this forlorn male. "I could keep you in exotic fruits," she cooed.

"Hah," he said. "None of that fancy stuff for me. I like grass. Nice, cool grass."

Pipi shares her nest with Mel now.

If you were to observe Pipi and Mel today, you would see two love birds cooing. One has a relatively large brain, keen sight, a twenty-two-inch wing span, and a short, stout body covered with heavy brown plumage. And the other has similar attributes, except, of course, for the usual sexual differences. They probably look quite equal to you. Yet one flies over high mountains, across the grand oceans, to the far corners of the world. And the other stays in the pigeonhole and hardly flutters his wings.

Pipi feels whole again. Mel isn't much of a bird, but it didn't take much to make Pipi feel complete—she is so big on her own. She regurgitates for Mel varied grasses that she collects from distant shores, and she tells him tales of her great adventures. He listens and he keeps her warm at night. And that is enough for her.

**MORAL**

**Never pigeonhole a pigeon.**

# GOOSE GODDESS

When all the young geese went off to the universities to learn how to function in their sophisticated land, Gertie stayed in the barnyard. "I'm not sending you to college to become a bum," said Papa Goose.

Gertie was raised like an old-fashioned goose. She was raised to love her mommy and daddy. She was taught to clean the barnyard and to make vegetable stews. Her cleaning was most thorough and her stews won accolades from the barnyard fowls, but Gertie's accomplishments didn't make her happy. She felt silly being the only young goose in the barnyard.

"Mating with Gertie would be like mating with my mother," said Harry Goose. "Gertie is not for this world," said James.

Mama gave up hope. "Life can be lived without your own gander," she told Gertie.

One day, a gander from the remotest part of the remotest mountain in the remotest range of mountains came to this sophisticated land. He came on a mission to sell the rare rhubarb that grew in his special corner of the world. He had another mission, too. He would bring back a mate who would be so sophisticated that he would be the envy of every male in his mountain.

He sold the local distributors plenty of rhubarb. And he met sisters and daughters of these ganders. None met his standards for the mate he would like to bring to his native land. Perhaps Dolly of Hello Dolly's Mating Service could help him.

Dolly's little brain began to click.

Her snow geese were off on the slopes.

Her blue geese were off singing the blues.

Her wild geese were off on a wild goose chase.

Her laughing geese were off goosing old ladies.

There was always Gertie Goose.

"Have I got a goose for you!" she honked.

Jeremy went to the barnyard to meet Gertie.

". . . but I cook," she said.

Jeremy's heart began to palpitate.

". . . and I clean," she said.

Tears welled up in Jeremy's eyes.

". . . and I love my mommy and daddy."

He began to tremble.

Then he noticed her callous-free feet. She was the only goose he had found with callous-free feet. "How come?" he asked in an unsteady voice. This would be the clincher.

She hung her head in shame. "I never left the yard."

Now Jeremy got goose bumps all over. He heard the answer he had hoped for. Here was the goddess of his dreams. A sophisticated goose who could live with the geese in his remote mountain. "Will you be my goose goddess?" he honked.

## GOOSE GODDESS

And so Gertie went to live in the remotest part of the remotest mountain in the remotest range of mountains—as a sophisticate.

---

### MORAL

**Who's to judge?**

---

# GUILT

"I will never be a mother like my mother," Maida promised herself. She would never tell her youngster, 'You're breaking my heart,' or, 'You're killing me.' She would let him follow his natural instincts and he would show her the right way a kangaroo should be brought up—the guilt-free way.

"When will you be ready to go to the fair, Maida?" William asked. William was her mate, the kangaroo that she loved.

"First, I have to groom our little one—you know he likes to be bathed at night," she said. "And then I'll play twinky-twinky toenails with him—our little cutie loves that. And then, you know, he likes to run around teasing the wallabies. And then I have to ask him how long he wants to stay up. Why don't you hop along, dear, and I'll meet you later at the fair."

William hopped off and Maida stayed at the home grounds with her little Conrad. She happily bathed him. She played twinky-twinky toenails with him. She let him chase the wallabies. And when he dived into her pouch head first and slid out as she relaxed her muscles, she said, "You're so adorable, Baby Doll." After he had dived in and slid out many times she said, "You're so much

107

# GUILT

friskier than all the other baby kangaroos I know. And there is a definite correlation between high energy and high intelligence. You're so bright! By the way, are you in for the night?"

In answer to her question, her little one slid out again.

Maida did and said all the right things, she was sure. She was a patient and loving mother. Her particular manner of care for her offspring made her feel exhausted most of the time, but she felt it was worth all her effort. Her goal was to have her little one feel no guilt, and if it killed her, Conrad would grow up with no guilt.

Maida had all but forgotten about the fair when Carmen stopped by and asked if she wanted to go there with her.

Maida turned to Conrad. "Are you in for the night yet?" she asked. And since he snorted out his words in a way that only his mother could understand, Maida interpreted his answer. "My little one says he may be in for the night. He's not sure. But he said it would disturb him to know that I'd be having a good time while he was sleeping in my pouch. I can't let him stay awake at the fair. He would want to go to the side show and there are horrors there that are so horrible they might traumatize him.

"Will you do me an elephant-size favor, Carmen? I'm supposed to meet my William at the fair. Will you tell him that I can't make it tonight? And another favor? Be a real friend and spend the evening with him so that he has company?"

Carmen promised to do Maida the favors she asked of her and hopped off to the fair. And Maida continued her joyous task of doing the right things for her little Conrad. "I don't mind not going places with your daddy. Honestly," she said. "And I want you to know, dear one, that no matter what any other kangaroo thinks, *I* am

108

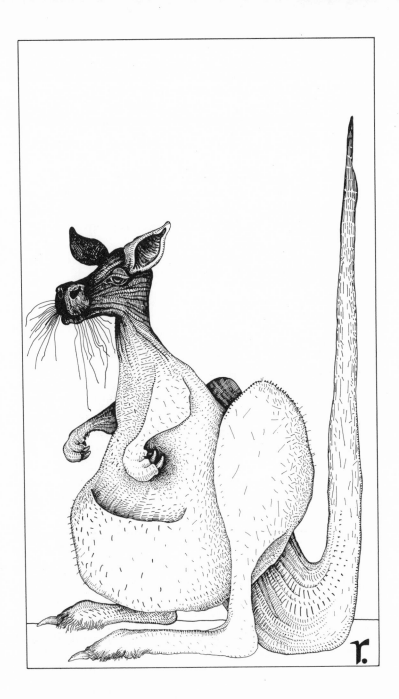

never embarrassed by your behavior. I know other kanga-roos can't understand my principles, but when you are grown up and have no guilt, no hang-ups, they will envy you and they will know I brought you up right. You don't know how darling you look splashing in the mud. You look just like a baby leopard. When will you be ready to hop in for the night?"

Around midnight, after Maida's little one had hopped in and slid out for the twentieth time, Carmen sauntered by. Carmen was in a happy mood, and sang:

> Oh, what a beautiful fair it was,
> And what a beautiful side show.
> A sheep with two heads,
> A fur-bearing chick,
> A goat with four horns,
> Enough to make you sick.
> And William brayed, "My love . . ."

"William said what?" Maida asked.

"Oh, he was so-o-o-o nice. He thanked me for spending the evening with him and, tee-hee, he said you ought to apply for a job at the freak show: You're the only kangaroo in the whole land who can't tame her little one. He asked me to meet him at the fair tomorrow. And there was something else . . . let me see if I can remember. Oh, yes. He asked me to tell you that he's moving in with me till little Conrad grows up."

"Lovely," said Maida absent-mindedly. By tuning in to Conrad constantly, Maida tuned out others. Carmen's words reached Maida's ears but not her awareness. Carmen hopped away satisfied that she had delivered her mes-sage. And Maida continued to give little Conrad her attention. She patted her pouch—he happened to be there at that moment—and looked into his big brown eyes with affection.

"No sacrifice is too much as long as it's for you,

Baby Doll," she said. And then realizing she had used one of the most guilt-producing words, she apologized. "Please forgive me," she cooed. "Nothing I do for you is a sacrifice. It is a privilege."

Maida dozed off, then woke up with a start. She grasped the full meaning of what Carmen had said to her. Her beloved William was moving out. He was moving in with Carmen. He was leaving her.

She owed her first loyalty to her little helpless one. No other kangaroo could take care of him. No kangaroo could understand him. He was worth every sacrifice. Yes, sacrifice, and that's what it was, a sacrifice, so she may as well call it by its correct name. She was sacrificing her young years, her marriage to her beloved William, for this little monster. Maybe he had been born a brat, but her enlightened guidance of him had hardly made him tolerable. She didn't want to leave her little Conrad. *But she didn't want to lose his father either.*

Without consciously planning her diatribe, the words came to her straight from her mother's mouth. "Do you know what you're doing to my life!" she yelped. "I sacrificed, yes, sacrificed everything for you and what do you do? You make my life a torture. You cause a breach between your father and me. I can't have a social life with you making all your demands on me. You're killing me. And I hope this gives you guilt, guilt, guilt. A little guilt never hurt any kangaroo, you tiger, you. If animals felt a little more guilt we wouldn't have so many killings. And let this be a warning: If you get out of my pouch again tonight, I will hate you as long as I live."

The next day, Maida arrived at the fair as it opened. When William arrived, fortunately before Carmen, Maida gave him a big hug.

"What's the matter with Conrad? He's so quiet. Is he sick?" he asked.

"Guilt. Oh, guilt, it's wonderful. William, would

you mind seeing the freak show again? I want Conrad to see it."

"It's not a pretty show. Are you sure you want him to see it?"

"It's time he learned some of the hazards of life," she said.

"You see that sheep with two heads, Conrad," said Maida at the freak show, "that's what happens to little ones when they give their mother aggravation."

"And this is what happens to you when you give me a normal life," said William, as he rubbed noses with his mate. "By the way, if Carmen gives you any message from me, I was only kidding."

Their little kangaroo is two now and he's growing by leaps and bounds. And, yes, he has as much guilt as the best of them.

---

## MORAL

**A little guilt never hurt anyone.**

---

# BABY BEAR GROWS UP

Once upon a time, not too long ago, there lived in a house deep in the woods a mama bear, a papa bear, and a baby bear. Every afternoon, the three bears would take a long walk together in the woods.

Mama would look at Baby, at her left, admiringly, and say something admiringly, like, "You whipped up a banquet this morning, my baby." That morning, Baby had burned the porridge.

And Papa would look at Baby, at his right, admiringly, and say something admiringly, like, "You float like a dream." Baby, as all could see, plunked about like a bear.

Baby looked at the ants crawling about. She felt as small as one of them. She knew she could never live up to Mama's and Papa's words of praise. But she had no need to live up to them. She could count on Mama and Papa for everything.

Baby Bear grew up, as baby bears will, and she had suitors.

There was Jack.

"He's too large," said Papa Bear.

"He's hardly full-sized," said Mama Bear.

"Then I guess he's not right," said Baby Bear. And she sent him on his way.

"Don't worry, don't worry, my baby," said Papa Bear."You can always count on us."

Then there was Jim.

"He's too fat," said Papa Bear.

"He's too lean," said Mama Bear.

"Then I guess he's not right," said Baby Bear. And she sent him on his way.

"Don't worry, don't worry, don't worry, my baby," said Mama Bear. "You can always count on us."

And then came Jonas.

"He growls too loudly," said Papa Bear.

"He hardly growls above a grunt," said Mama Bear.

"Then I guess he's not right," said Baby Bear. And she sent him on his way.

"Don't worry, Baby dear. Some day a bear will come who is worthy of you," said Papa Bear.

Baby Bear believed she had the best mama and papa in the woods. But there were those who believed otherwise. Little Bear Next Door, for one. "Your daddy wants you to be an old maid," she said.

Baby Bear rolled her tongue around in her mouth. "If I weren't a lady, I would have spat on you," she mumbled under her breath.

The years went by, and sad to tell, Papa Bear, as papa bears will, went to The Great Beyond.

And shortly thereafter, and sadly so, Mama Bear, as mama bears will, went to The Great Beyond.

And Baby Bear, poor Baby Bear, took her walks in the woods alone. She was lonely.

The suitors came, but they were few and far between. In fact, truth to tell, there was only one, Jonathan. He was in the blue bears' register.

But Baby Bear had learned her lesson well. "You're too rich for my blood. You're too poor in understanding of a bear of my background. There's many a babe in the woods who would drop dead over you. I guess you're not right," she said. And she sent him on his way.

Yet she knew that she would find a bear who was worthy of her. Didn't Mama and Papa tell her so?


The house in the woods was cold. And Baby felt cold. But she was proud, proud that she had maintained the standards that Papa Bear and Mama Bear had set for her.

One afternoon in the middle of July, she went for her accustomed walk in the woods. She passed the house of Little Bear Next Door. And, as she was rolling her tongue about in her mouth, thinking of the spit she would like to have spat if she weren't a lady, she heard some gleeful shouts. She peeked out of her right eye and looked in the direction of the house of Little Bear Next Door. She saw Little Bear Next Door playing kick football with her mate and their three little cubs. "Crass," muttered Baby Bear under her breath.

Baby Bear went back to her house in the woods. It seemed to her to be colder than it had ever been before. So cold that even the largest roaring fire she could make did not take the chill out of the house.

She heard a knock at the door. She peeked through a slit and saw a bear standing outside who was larger than any bear should be, and hardly full-sized; he was too fat, and rather lean; he seemed too rich, and he had a hole in his sock—he looked a mess. "Who is there?" she called.

And with a loud growl that sounded hardly more than a grunt, he replied, "It is I, The Caller. I am a suitor seeking your paw with the intentions of matrimony."

"Just one moment," she called out in the sexiest voice she could manage.

She plunked about the room. Her paws fluttered. "What shall I do? What shall I do?" she said, addressing the flame in the fireplace. And, as she looked at the flame, she thought she saw Papa. Yes, that was him. He looked just right. And that was Mama beside him. She looked just right, too. No, there was something not right about them. She'd better talk to them.

"Listen, Papa. It's cold outside. But it's colder inside, much colder. And it's cold in my heart—you can't imagine how cold. And you may as well hear this and hear it straight. I'm no better than any baby bear. And Mama's a drag and you mated with her. Yes, Mama, you really are a drag. And Papa's a drag and you mated with him. And you're both a drag on me. I don't want to die wondering. I want a warm body beside me. You can't tell me how to live any more. There's going to be a hot time in this old house tonight and this old block of ice is going to melt."

And she blew a cobweb down from the weathered ceiling and placed it in front of her eyes. She reached for some stardust and mixed it in with the cobweb. She sucked in her belly and turned up the corners into a smile. And she prayed that he would find her worthy of him.

Well, he found her worthy.

There are bears in the woods who think Baby has gone mad, for every time the name of Mama Bear or Papa

Bear is mentioned in her presence, Baby rolls her tongue about in her mouth.

## MORAL

**Sometimes any mate can make baby happier than no mate at all.**

# RECOGNITION

"My daddy said I can't go on the Duck Walk Friday night if I don't finish my homework," cried Bonnie Duck, "and it's impossible to finish it by then."

"Why don't you just tell him you finished it?" said Annie Duck. "He'll never know."

"But you don't know my daddy. He checks on everything. I don't know why Professor Goat wants me to write about the Rent Wars anyway. He knows all about them already and I don't want to know about them at all."

"The Rent Wars?" quacked Annie. "You lucked out, Bon. I wrote a paper on that last week and you can have it if you want."

Bonnie didn't mind ducking a little work. She looked at the paper. It seemed to cover the subject. The two ducks went to different schools. Bonnie was a student at Professor Goat's School for Ducks at the north end of the farm, and Annie was a student at Professor Sheep's School for Ducks at the south end of the farm. The friends reasoned that both professors were so absent-minded that if they should meet by chance and one professor would show the other professor the paper, neither professor would remember that he had read it before. And Bonnie *had* to go on the walk.

"I'll take it," she said. "And thanks."

"Anything for a friend," said Annie.

The next time the two ducks met, Bonnie was not so appreciative. "I could kill you," she said.

"What did I do?" asked Annie.

"It's that lousy paper. Why didn't you tell me it was that good? The old goat put my article in the *Goat School Annual*. He gave me the cover story and put my picture on the cover and he's entering it in the county contest. And I have to live with this thing. Lauded for something I never did. I feel terrible."

Annie apologized, "It was only a C paper and I just wanted you to be able to go on the Walk."

Professor Sheep and Professor Goat did meet several months later at the combined graduation ceremony of the North School and the South School. As professors sometimes will, they discussed their students.

"It never fails," said Professor Sheep. "I can pick them all the time. You see that duck over there? That's Annie. The first week of school she submitted a paper on the Rent Wars. It was a disaster. She didn't dot the I's or cross the T's and she couldn't stay within the margins at all. That duck would never amount to anything, I knew. I gave her a C out of the generosity of my heart. And just as I had judged her, that duck never did amount to anything."

"Yup," said Professor Goat. "Funny, I can pick them all the time, too. You see that duck getting the honors now? That's Bonnie. I recognized her merit, coincidentally, when *she* submitted a paper on the Rent Wars. It was creative, original. I didn't want such talent to dissipate so I gave her the lead article in our magazine. Every time I saw her I said, 'How's our Writer Laureate today?' I gave her something to live up to and she hasn't disappointed me. She was just offered a job as editor of *Today's Duck*."

"You've got all the luck," said Professor Sheep. "They always give me the dumb ducks."

"I guess I *am* lucky," said Professor Goat.

## MORAL

**Tell her she's wonderful.**

# FISH STORY

"Now you be good little fishies," Sacrificing said. "I'm going upstream to lay some eggs."

"You can get killed there, Ma," said Yellow Yolk.

Sacrificing swam upstream, and you can guess what dreadful end she came to.

"Taking the high stream gets you up a creek," said Sexy. "I'll take the low."

"No big fish would swim in low, low streams," said Yellow Yolk. "Besides, Mama would turn over in her watery grave if she knew she sacrificed her life for a fish with a low-down life like yours."

"Shut your gills, Yellow Belly. Where did Ma end up with her good-fish life! If a fish is old enough and tired enough, he'd swim in low waters."

"He'd have to be half-dead," said Yellow Yolk.

"That's the best kind," said Sexy. "The sooner to get his golden bowl."

And she took the low stream to look for a big fish who would take care of her.

Sexy opened up a nursery school low-stream, Little Nursery School For Little Fish of Means. She had lovely

toys for the fish to play with, bridges to swim under, and swings to swing on. On the surface her school looked good, and she filled it with little fish easily.

Sexy declared every Monday Granddaddy's Day. And each Monday, Sexy asked a different little fish to invite her graddaddy to visit the school.

Mindy was the first. Alas, Mindy brought her mama instead. After watching Sexy teach, Mindy's mama said that Sexy shouldn't give her little minnows ideas of swimming in big ponds. "And how did you get in our stream anyway! And what is your pedigree!"

Sexy was not discouraged. She would try again.

The next little fish to invite her granddaddy was Goldie Goldfish. Granddaddy Goldfish felt the school did not have the scholarly atmosphere that Goldie's mother was led to believe it had. "I don't want my virgin grandchild in your catfish house any more," he said. And he took Goldie out of the school.

But Sexy did not lose heart. After all, she needed only one big fish to give her the golden bowl she craved. She would try again.

The next week, Sexy asked Little Sally Salmon to bring her granddaddy. Little Sally began to cry. "My granddaddy can hardly swim. He is so old and he is smoked. He is more dead than alive."

"You lucky little one," said Sexy. That is the best kind. You must bring him in. If you need any help, I'll come and get him."

"I'll try," said little Sally. And Monday afternoon, as the sun was setting, little Sally brought her granddaddy in. And truly, he was more dead than alive. He huffed like a submarine that was losing its thrust. His tail barely flapped. His gills sucked in and spewed out the water so slowly that he seemed to be semicomatose.

# FISH STORY

"You look rather familiar, Madam," said Granddaddy Smokey. "Are you perchance one of the pickled fishes I met slobbering about the bar at the coral reef?"

Sexy acted offended. "At the bar? At the coral reef?" She repeated Granddaddy Smokey's words as if she would never think of going to a bar, nor even to the coral reef. "We low-stream swimmers *do* things today." And she added impressively, "I'm in enterprise."

Little Sally's granddaddy was impressed. "Is this your enterprise?" he asked admiringly.

"Yes," said Sexy, making a modest graceful twirl.

"How enterprising!" he said.

"Yes, this is my school. I believe in taking care of myself. I don't believe in baiting big fish." Now she waved her fins and dragged her tail forward sexily.

And Granddaddy Smokey looked at Sexy's waving, sexy fins and he looked at her sexily dragging tail. What a catch, he thought. And such a sexy fish. And she doesn't believe in baiting big fish. And she believes in taking care of herself. And she has her own enterprise, a scholarly school. "Will you share my golden bowl?" he asked.

## MORAL

**There is no fish like an old fish.**

# THE BEAVER AND
# THE CRAB

Barnett was a beaver who owned a successful restaurant, and he had a son who wanted to be a successful restaurateur. So he sent his son to the School of Hotel Administration, and when Junior graduated he said, "Papa, now I know how to run a restaurant."

"What did you learn in school, my son?" asked Barnett.

"I learned that you must present things well in order to have your guests want them. For example, look at your menu. You should never say 'Dead Duck.' That's terrible."

"What would you say, Junior?" asked Barnett.

"I would call it *Canard rôti comme il faut à la mode.*"

"Oh? I'm willing to learn. I will write up a new menu and benefit from your education, too." And he wrote up a new menu and asked his son to present it to the first customer who came in.

As fate would have it, Mr. Crab was the first customer. Barnett was pleased. He thought it would be good experience for his son.

Junior greeted Mr. Crab warmly (as he had been taught to do in school), showed him to a center table (as

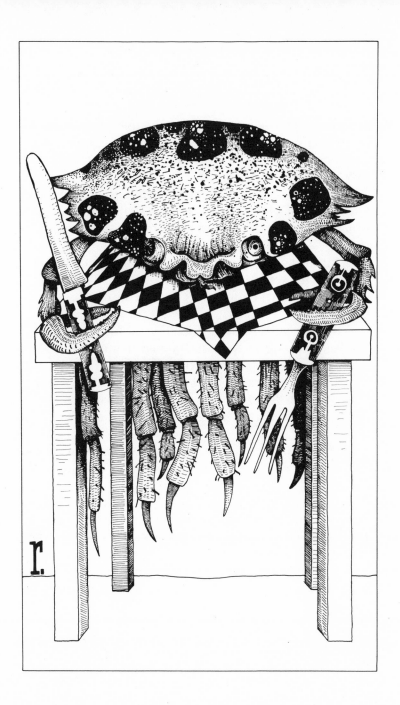

r.

he had been taught to seat important patrons), seated him facing the door, and gave him the new menu. Mr. Crab ordered the *Canard rôti comme il faut à la mode* and Junior was delighted. He looked in his father's direction for approval, and his father nodded in approval.

Then he turned to Mr. Crab. "That will take at least fifty minutes," said Junior.

"Fifty minutes! Why, in less time than that I can have a session with my analyst, write a letter to my mother, pinch an old lady's toe, and make love. I won't wait. I'm leaving. And that's final."

Junior had learned that he could expect crabby customers. Oh, well, those were the breaks. There would always be another customer. He hoped the next one would be a bunny.

But Barnett saw Mr. Crab slide off his seat, with his ten legs tapping in a most agitated manner, and walk down the aisle toward the exit door. Barnett had learned that a restaurant was as good as its last satisfied customer, and Mr. Crab didn't look like a satisfied customer. Something must be wrong. He had better find out what was going on.

"Fifty minutes!" continued Mr. Crab. "One would think I had nothing better to do. I'm a very busy crab, you know."

"Fifty minutes? Why, my dear Mr. Crab, you won't have to wait at all. Why don't you have a drink while I get your order? We make the driest Raven's Bloody Mary this side of the Falls."

Mr. Crab took a sip of the drink offered him. "I can't wait and I won't wait," he said. But he finished his cocktail.

"May I suggest an order of crisp seaweed? Our house is famous for it." The cocktail had calmed Mr. Crab down a bit and he agreed to have the seaweed.

"A salad comes with the duck, Mr. Crab. Our finest clients always have their salad before the duck."

"Well, then, why do you ask? Am I not as good as your finest clients?" Mr. Crab ate the salad.

"And now you must have lemon sherbert to clear the palate." Mr. Crab ate the lemon sherbert.

As soon as Mr. Crab had finished the lemon sherbert and fifty minutes after Barnett had taken Mr. Crab's order, he served him, with a grand flourish, the *Canard rôti comme il faut à la mode*. It was a great success. Mr. Crab said it was the finest *Canard rôti comme il faut à la mode* he had ever had and promised to tell all his friends about it. He found time to smoke an after-dinner weed, and was seen dancing a happy jig as he was leaving the establishment.

"How did you do it, Papa?" Junior asked later. "I told him it would take at least fifty minutes and it did, and when I told him it would take fifty minutes he was ready to walk out."

"It's just as you learned in school, son. It's all in the way you present it."

### MORAL

**It's all in the way you say it.**

# THE PHILOSOPHIC
# OATH

Olga was an ostrich who became a philosopher bird.
Ozzie was an ostrich who became a medical bird.

They were colorless, timid creatures and in their fear
of facing the world, they clung to each other in a state
that they believed was . . . .

"I love you very much," said Ozzie.

"And I love you more than that," said Olga.

"Do you love me even though I hardly mix with
other birds?" asked Ozzie.

"I love you even though . . . Ozzie?"

"What is it, my long-necked one?"

"I have a philosophy. I never want you to be bored,
or to feel restricted or tied down. I want you to feel free to
go any place, with any creature, any time you feel the
urge."

"I just want to be with you, my big-thighed one, and
you alone."

"Let's take a philosophic oath that you are free to go
wheresoever you want, whensoever, and with whomso-
ever."

# THE PHILOSOPHIC OATH

"If you will take the same oath," he said.

And they both took the philosophic oath and they became mates.

If one were to approach their pit, one would have to be quite close to see that there were two ostriches—they always seemed like one. One would hear Ozzie ask, "How do you feel, my darling?" And Olga would reply, "I feel well, really well." But Ozzie couldn't be sure that she truly felt well, so he would put his stethoscope to her breast to check her medically. Now the mere touch of the stethoscope to Olga's breast made her feel ill, and when he would ask her again how she felt, she would say, "I feel ill."

Ozzie tried to determine the cause for her ill feelings, but was unable to. He used his stethoscope again and again in the hope that that would help him make a diagnosis. Ozzie felt good when Olga felt ill, for he could then prove his love for her by doctoring her. "We'll both stay close to our sand pit, my long-legged one, and worry together about your health."

That upset Olga. "You must go out and mix with other birds," she said. "I am not good company for you when I am ill."

"But I want to stay by your side," he said.

Olga kept urging him to go, telling him there were other sick birds who needed his care, reminding him of his philosophic vows, but she couldn't persuade him to leave her.

When Olga felt well again, she praised Ozzie for his extraordinary doctoring ability and after several episodes of Olga's illness and recovery, followed by Olga's extravagant compliments of Ozzie's extraordinary abilities, Ozzie began to feel there *was* something extraordinary about his doctoring abilities and something extraordinarily extraordinary about himself. He was no longer the timid creature afraid to face the world. So one evening, when Olga said, "Why should a great medical bird like you break our philosophic vows, especially tonight when there is a very important meeting of medical birds from many fields," Ozzie said, "I'll go."

Olga thought unhappy thoughts while he was away to help her keep her level of sickness. She wanted him to have the pleasure of helping her feel better when he returned.

"How are you, my two-toed wonder?" Ozzie asked.

"Not well," she said, "but no worse than before. Did you have a good time, dear?"

"I worried about you all the time I was away," he said. "In fact, I discussed your case all evening with Gloria."

"Gloria?" she asked. "Who is Gloria?"

"Oh, a fine medical bird who is famous for her diagnoses. In fact, I have arranged to spend the weekend with her to discuss your case further. Are you sure you want me to go? I won't go if you don't want me to."

She assured him it was all right and told him he was simply living up to their vows. "But will you examine me before you leave?" she asked, for she felt a gnawing feeling in her breast that was a new feeling for her.

Ozzie took out his stethoscope. Then he looked at his beloved. He put his stethoscope down. He laughed. "I don't need this to make my diagnosis tonight, my dear." He nuzzled her affectionately. "My diagnosis is— that you are jealous. I won't leave you tonight, my love. I'll stay with you."

Jealous? thought Olga. Impossible! But no, it was not impossible. It seemed possible to her now that she was jealous of this fat-ass predatory female who was trying to take her Ozzie away from her. But she had lived by her philosophy. She couldn't abandon it now. "Me, jealous?" "Impossible! she said. There is no place in my philosophy for jealousy, my love."

Ozzie went to meet Gloria. He runs around with her today, but Olga doesn't want to see that, so she keeps her head in the sand.

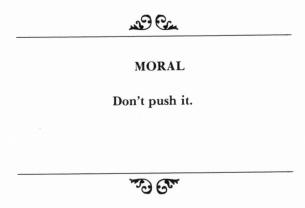

## MORAL

**Don't push it.**

# ALTERNATE LIFE STYLE

Mother Goose raised her brood. Knew how to stretch an ear of corn. Knew how to save some seeds for a rainy day.

"Why don't you put your seeds in my name, Ma," said Daughter Goose, "then the government will pay."

"Pay?" asked Mother Goose. "Pay for what?"

"Pay for the nursing barn for the rest of your life," said Daughter. "It's the latest thing."

"Neh, neh, neh," said Mother. She was interested in some of the latest things, but positively not in that. She remembered when Aunt Kitty went to live in the nursing barn and put her seeds in her daughter's name. After a time, Aunt Kitty wanted to leave the barn and her daughter said, 'You can't afford to be on your own. You have no seeds.' And when Aunt Dora, who had never saved a seed, wanted to live on her own in her old age, she had to beg for crumbs.

There were better ways for Mother Goose to finish her life. She would put her seeds to work. She had better hurry.

She said 'Goodbye' to Daughter Goose, cried a bucket of tears, and filled a bag with her belongings.

She went to see her old friends to present her new plan.

"So you want me to join your commune? Absolutely not. I'd rather be hit with a *knoedle* than take off my girdle. Sex, sex, sex, that's what communes are all about. I know," said Straight Lace.

"I can't go to a commune," said Proper Goose. "I suffer from terminal helplessness. Pardon me, but I have to leave now for The Gone Goose Barn. Of course, I gave my seeds to my daughter. What kind of a mother do you think I am?"

She had better luck with Loosey Goose. "They say I have a screw loose anyway. What have I got to lose?" And Aida Goose: "God helps those who help themselves. I'm ready to join." And Ducky Goose: "I never fit into this technological society anyway. Count me in."

The four cronies searched for a place to start their commune. They found a place they thought perfect, an abandoned farm near the end of Boggs Road. They planted their seeds and grew cabbages and onions, cauliflower and corn, and many roses, red and white. Their bellies were full and their hearts were full, too. They would show their thanks to God of All Creatures for the good harvest he had provided by giving gifts of love to those who would accept them.

They placed a sign in the middle of the road with an arrow that pointed to their commune: "Detour, Construction, Big Giveaway Special Today." When the cars stopped, the geese each tossed a rose to the driver and each goose honked a message of love: "Lovers make better neighbors," "Lovers make better pickles," "When you are loved you smell roses," "Don't eat garlic if you want to be loved."

One visitor was not amused. "This property is the

property of the survivors of old Henry Boggs," he said. "And you're not them." He showed his badge. The town policeman! "You must leave at once or you will be charged with the crime of trespassing."

Crime? They had never been in trouble with the law before and Mother Goose could not see this as a crime. She had worked too hard to create this lifestyle to give up without a fight. "Where are the survivors?" she asked. "If they want us to leave, they can tell us so. And who says this property ever belonged to old Henry? God left this land for *all* his creatures and I don't think God would want us to leave."

"How do you old geese live, anyway?" asked the policeman. "Are you on welfare?"

Mother Goose was indignant. "We grow our own," she said proudly.

"Now, don't give me a hard time. You old biddies belong in the nursing barn. Your heads shake; your necks hang like turkey necks; you move as slow as snails. You all look so terrible, I can't stand to look at you."

"If it hurts you so much to look at us, lovey, why don't you close your eyes?" said Mother Goose.

"What a lovely thought," said Loosey. "Now let's all sing together." And to the tune of "The Old Grey Mare," the four little old geese sang:

> Close your eyes
> And you won't have to look at us,
> Won't have to look at us,
> Won't have to look at us.
> Close your eyes
> And you won't have to look at us
> Many long years to come.

The policeman closed his eyes and thought. He had closed his eyes to many a thing in his day. His retirement was coming up. He wouldn't want to go to a nursing home himself. Maybe these old geese had a good idea. "Hey, cuties, if anyone asks, I didn't see a thing," he said. And he winked his eye, waved his hand, and drove away.

**MORAL**

**There are alternatives, Mother.**

# AN ASS IS AN ASS

"Ginny says she loves me, Daddy, and she wants to get hitched."

Daddy looked at his scrawny, dull-colored, big-eared, scrubby-maned, lazy runt of a son. "Don't be asinine, my son," he said, "She's only after my grain."

And Jack, the ass, told Ginny. "My daddy said you are after his grain."

"I love you so much," she said, "that if we get hitched I will bring in the scrub for you. Let's, huh?" She was an ass, too.

"She said she'll bring in the scrub for me, Daddy."

"Don't be a ninny. Why should she labor for an ass like you?"

"Why?" she answered Jack in reply to his daddy's question. "Because, my silly ass, I love you. And because you are gifted. Your brays are so loud and sustained, and they dip to the flattest flats. I want you never to get your nose wet, never to have to get your feet in the mud. I want you to be able to roll in the grass, to be able to create your songs and sing them without worry. I want to nurture your genius. Someday the whole animal world will acclaim you, I know. I want to forage for you. I would rather feed you than feed myself."

And when Jack told his dad that Ginny would rather feed him than feed herself, he replied, "What kind of cock-and-bull story is that! No jenny would do without in order to feed a jackass."

Jack was an ass, but he was not a complete ass. He and Ginny got hitched.

And when Jack told his dad, Daddy said, "Not a grain of grain from me. We'll see how she likes that."

How did Ginny like that? She liked it fine. She liked to roam through the highlands and the lowlands, gathering thistle tops and willow branches and hawthorn shoots for Jack. And she liked to bray about him wherever she roamed.

"I know a singer—he's sensational. He does bluegrass with folk-flavored feeling. He does sentimental ballads, torchy confessionals, novelty ditties. He can do progressive rock, new wave rock, and funk-country rock. He is a genuine genius. I have an 'in' with him and I think I can talk him into singing with your band."

She brayed to the horses and to the mountain goats. She brayed to the oxen and to the sheep. She interpreted the slightest flicker of their eyes as a possibility, and the slightest possibility of a possibility as encouragement to persist. And she persisted. She listened to Jack's songs and cheered him on. "Some band will give you a break soon," she said. "You'll see."

Her persistence brought results: "How can I say 'no' to you," said Lum Ox. He told Ginny he would engage Jack for the Harvest Festival with his Satan's Rollers.

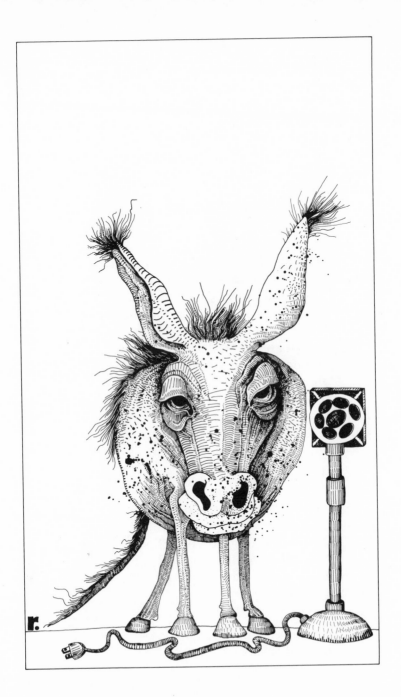

Bessie would not be out-done. She asked Ginny to use her influence to get Jack for the hoedown for her Cow's Moo. Soon, bands high in the highlands and low in the lowlands fought to have Jack sing with them. They all thought he was terrific.

The grain rolled in. Jack became the most famous donkey in his field. He was happy. He had made it. He was a star.

Ginny was happy. She had made him make it. And she was hitched to a star.

Daddy was not so happy. "You know, Jack, you come from a very fine family," he said.

"I know that," said Jack.

"And you are a donkey of achievement," said Daddy.

"I know that, I know that, Daddy," said Jack.

"Now we are a genteel family. A family of refinement. We are a good family, well-mannered and considerate."

"Oh, yes, Daddy. I know that," said Jack.

"Now Jack, I would like to ask you: What kind of a half-ass are you to be hitched to a pushy ninny like Ginny? You know she *is* pushy."

"My daddy says you're pushy," said Jack.

"But of course," said Ginny.

"Do you mean to say that you don't deny you're pushy?"

"Of course I mean to say—I'll say it loud and clear: I'm pushy. And I won't deny it. I *am* pushy. And that's the truth. Do you think you would be heard today if I weren't pushy?"

Jack spoke to Daddy.
And Daddy spoke to Jack.

# AN ASS IS AN ASS

And now they both agreed that Jack was too important a donkey to be hitched to a pushy mate. Jack unhitched himself from Ginny. She kicked him. She bit him with fury. "I've been a stupid ass," she screeched at him. And indeed she had been.

But an ass can learn. And Ginny learned. She became a smart ass. And before the frost got off the ground, she found a dumb donkey who was willing to forage for her. And she and Don got hitched.

Oh—and Jack? For a while his grain rolled in. And then it stopped. No more calls for him to perform, for alas, the public was fickle, as the public can be. Did you think he would be called if Ginny weren't there to push him? Oh, yes—and Daddy says that the reason Jack failed is that an ass is an ass.

## MORAL

**An ass is still an ass.**

# DON'T WORRY

Warren was a worrybird. He worried. He worried about the rain. He worried about the grain. He worried about other commodities. He worried about all futures.

Wilma was a worrybird. She worried, too. She worried about Warren. She worried about whether she would please him; she worried about whether he would leave her. And now she had a new worry—ohmigod, why did she ever do it?—she worried that he would find out. And if he found out, he would surely squawk. He would squawk loud. He might even holler, holler very loud, holler very, very loud. She worried: What would he do after he squawked and hollered if he found out? She knew he squawked when she forgot what she was supposed to remember; and he squawked when she remembered what she was supposed to forget. But she had never done such a daring thing before. What would he do?

"The frost is on the pumpkin, Wilma," he said. "Time to fly south."

Wilma knew she was supposed to pack their satchel. She knew she was supposed to pack his snorkel, a bit of seed, some suntan oil, and some salt-water protective. She packed.

"Did you check?" asked Warren.

"Of course," she said. And she did check.

"Are you sure?" he asked.

# DON'T WORRY

"Yes. I counted the items," she said. And she had indeed counted the items: one, two, three, four. But when she counted, she counted the satchel as an item. She did not remember that she had never counted the satchel as an item before.

The pair of worrybirds flew south.

"You're quite a bird, Wilma," said Warren. "Now for a good swim. Snorkel!"

Wilma opened the satchel. She looked for the snorkel. Alas, the snorkel was not there.

"Oh, Warren," she peeped, "I'm sorry. I'm *so* sorry. If it were something of my own that I had left behind, I wouldn't care. But—yours . . . I feel terrible. Look, I'll fly back north. I'll pick up your snorkel. I'll have it here tomorrow." As she said it, her knees wobbled, her feathers fluttered, she trembled all over.

Warren looked at her with disgust. "Do you mean to say you would fly all the way north to carry back my snorkel? FORGET IT. It's too late. Some mistakes cannot be corrected. You made a mistake you cannot correct."

"I feel so terrible, Warren," she peeped.

"You feel terrible? You should. You feel terrible because you're dumb. You know you're dumb. I know you're dumb. You know I know you're dumb," said Warren, and he lay down on the sand, put his beak under his wing, and slumped over into a heavy slumber.

Wilma trembled from the tip of her beak to the tip of her claws. She felt dumb. She rolled her feathered body into a ball and wished she could die. If Warren squawked so when he learned she forgot to bring his snorkel, what would he do when he found out? How he would holler! How he would squawk and shriek. Wilma let out a mournful cry, "I want to die!" she cried. She lay prostrate. She waited. She did not die.

But she had to die. There was no other solution for her. Wait! She had a solution. She would leave Warren. If she left him, she would surely die. She would die of loneliness. But that would be better than listening to his hollering. She would leave him.

She flapped her wings and flew a few yards and fell to the ground. She must be dead. This must be what death was like.

She cried for the poor little worrybird who used to be. She cried for poor Warren—how lost he would be without her. She cried for all little worrybirds who were lost and gone forever.

Wilma felt the warm tears on her cheeks. If she felt their liquid warmth, she knew that she could not be dead.

"I must die," she cried. "I absolutely must die." But she still didn't die. "I know how I can die," she thought. "I will fly back to Warren. I will tell him all about what I did. He will squawk. He will holler loud. He will screech so loud that he will cause an explosion of thunder and the earth will part. And when the earth parts, I will fall in and die. And I will never have to worry about Warren's squawking—I'll never have to worry about his hollering, or his screeching any more. He will holler at me, of course, but it will be his last holler."

She nudged Warren. "Warren, I have something to tell you," she peeped.

"What could you tell me? You had the snorkel under your wing all the time?"

"No, not that. It's something else."

"You had an affair? Ha! Who would have an affair with you?"

"No," she peeped. She pulled her feathers close and stiffened her body to prepare herself for the holocaust. She shivered. She shook. "I-I-I've invested some seed in a new product," she chirped with nervous speed (get the words out quickly so she could have a speedy end). "It's a worrybird ring. When worrybirds think things are going well for them, they turn the worrybird ring and they are reminded of catastrophes that have happened in the past, and they are reminded, too, that catastrophes will happen in the future." Then poor Wilma shivered some more and shook, shook, shook, shook, shook, and she peeped with her smallest peep the words that would end it all for her: "I invested—I invested with my own seed."

"You wouldn't have the nerve," squawked Warren. "You're dumb, but not that dumb. You know your seed is my seed. And you know no worrybird has to be reminded to worry—he can do that all by himself." He narrowed his eyes and he looked at Wilma skeptically, "Besides, if there were something new on the market, I would be the first to hear it—my hearing is the keenest. There is no worrybird ring."

"Oh, yes there is, Warren. And I did it. I cannot tell a lie."

"There is a worrybird ring?"

"Yes, there is, Warren. Please . . . please . . ."

"And you did it?"

"I didn't mean any harm, Warren. Our little ones have flown. And all the mother birds are doing things today . . ."

"And you used my seed?"

"Bu–bu–but your seed is my seed? Isn't your seed my seed?"

And then it began.

Warren squawked.

He shrieked.

He hollered.

He squawked and shrieked and hollered so loud that . . . . Oh yes, poor Wilma, it was happening now. Just as she had hoped and feared. There were rumbling sounds from the heavens. In just one minute there would be an explosion of thunder. Soon the earth would part. Wilma would happily fall in and die. And little worrybirds who had hardly had their chance in life to worry would die, too. Oh, what had she done!

The rumbling sounds got louder and louder. Rrrrrrrr. But there was no explosion, nor thunder, nor did the earth part. All the worrybirds for miles around came to find out what the big commotion was all about. They flew in in one dark cloud and the sound of the wings of the thousands of anxious birds sounded like the rumble of thunder.

"What's all the squawking about?" asked Moaner. He was the leader of the flock.

"She did it!" shrieked Warren. "She made a worrybird ring and she used my seed."

Amazing news. The flock was silenced. Then they chirped in unison, "A worrybird ring?"

"A worrybird ring! Yes, a worrybird ring. Turn it and it reminds you what to worry about," squawked Warren. "Did you ever hear such nonsense?"

The worrybirds bought all the rings Wilma had made.

Now, friends, I know you'll be happy to know that Wilma did not die, nor did she want to die any more. Of course, she still worries—well, she's a worrybird, isn't she? She still worries about Warren, but she doesn't worry, will he leave me? Instead, she worries, will he keep screeching long enough and loud enough so the worrybirds will keep coming to buy the rings?

---

**MORAL**

**Fear of fighting keeps many a birdie on her perch.**

---

# A MOST UNCOMMON
# BUTTERFLY

Mama Butterfly looked upon a lettuce leaf one day and said, "I do believe I've laid an egg." She watched the egg until the shell cracked and a crawling creature broke out of the shell. "Ah, a caterpillar!" she said. "Soon he will be the most perfect flying gem, a most extraordinary butterfly."

No, Mama Butterfly didn't have any special insight into what this little bugger would become. But Mama Butterfly was a mama, and mamas everywhere believe that the creature they have given birth to is Something Special.

"Ma, I want some water," said little Monarch.

Now Mama Butterfly thought that Monarch was Something Special and she wanted him to have the things she never had when she was young. So she brought him some special Vichy water from the springs of Vichy.

"Hm," thought Monarch, "my mom is weak." For Monarch, like little crawlers everywhere, could spot a mom on whom he could put something over.

# A MOST UNCOMMON BUTTERFLY

"Wine, Mama. I think I want some wine." And Mama Butterfly thought, "My poor baby has no papa and I want him to have a better life than I." And so she flew to the finest vineyards in the south of France and brought Monarch some vintage wine.

"I need a silken cloak for my true love," he said. And Mama saved the nectar from the tulips and bought her son a silken cloak for his lady love.

Now Monarch knew that he was boss. What were his limits? Maybe the sky. He would try. "I want a cabana on the Riviera," he said. "I need to bask in the sun. And Mama Butterfly got him a cabana on the Riviera, and gave him plenty of lettuce, and said, "Enjoy yourself, my son. You're Something Special and I want the best for you."

"Don't you think." said Kalma Butterfly, "that it is time your little crawler shed his skin? Even the Giant Swallowtail, who grows to a most enormous size, would have shed his skin by now."

"He is a most uncommon caterpillar," said Mama Butterfly. "No doubt you know that those who are the most highly developed, be they mammal, insect, or bird, take the greatest length of time to mature. There is plenty of time for my little crawler."

"Why don't you have Monarch gather leaves like other caterpillars do?" asked Vicki Butterfly. "The weatherman predicts an early frost."

"My son is meant for better things," she said.

She knew someday he would be a king among the butterflies. She bought him a seat in the Butterfly School of Public Administration, a blue canvas schoolbag, and a new shirt and tie. "Time for school," she said.

By now, poor Monarch not only fooled his mother, but also fooled himself. He knew all creatures large and

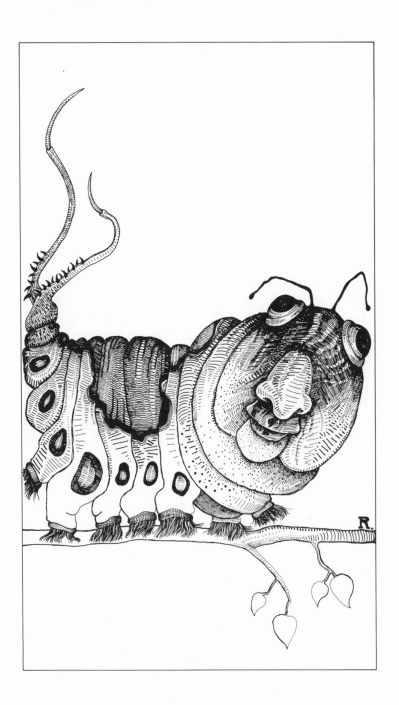

small have to learn to get along in the world. But he believed he was Something Special. "Not yet, Mama," he said. "I have to bask in the sun."

Alas, one sad day a little girl who always got butter-flies before exams came with a butterfly net and captured poor Mama.

Monarch gathered together a cluster of butterflies. "Who will adopt me?" he asked.

"You're much too old," said Vicki Butterfly. "Why don't you shed your skin and fly and get your own nectar?" she asked.

"It's been on my back so long that it has adhered. It's stuck. It's glued. And my mama never taught me how to fly, and I don't have a Ph.D. or an LL.B. or an M.D. And I never had a papa to pay my bills and make me go to school like you."

He went to a social service investigator. "Is there no medicare or medicaid or any other kind of aid for me?" he asked.

"You are much too young for that, my crawling friend. And you're strong enough to work. What can you do?"

"I prepared to wear the crown," he said. "And crawled around. And loved all creatures large and small, and—" he added proudly, "I am most charming at a cocktail party . . ."

"You can get your own lettuce," said Social Service.

And Monarch crawled about and begged for food and there were those who said that they thought Monarch was not a caterpillar at all. He crawled just like a worm.

Perhaps Weak-Winged Wilma would heed his pleas: "My mama-dear was kind to you," he said. "She loved me, so she worked her wings off to feed me with a silver spoon. You could repay her for past kindnesses by taking care of me." Wilma gave him some drippings from the nectar she had gathered. But they were not enough to sustain him.

My ma would have fed me better than this, he thought. But, of course, my ma isn't here any more. And I am so dry and the rumblings in my stomach bother me, so I must do something about it. And he made a decision contrary to any decision he had ever made in his life: He would feed himself.

He nibbled on an ivy leaf and then on the leaf of a rose. And then he chewed on a lettuce leaf. And a natural yet astonishing thing happened. He began to grow, and he grew so large that he burst out of his cocoon. "I am a butterfly," he said proudly. "And I can wing it on my own now!"

Was he a Painted Lady, or a Roadside Skipper, or a Mourning Cloak, or a Silvery Blue, or a Common Wood Nymph? No! Was he a Southern Dogface or a Common Anglewing? No! But he was better than a caterpillar. And far, far better than a worm. He was an ordinary Morpho Rhetnor. And that, my dear friends, is a creditable butterfly. Quite.

## MORAL

**Look ma, no hands.**

# FIRST ONE IN
# IN THE MORNING

Possum was a possum who loved to play. And he could well afford to play, he believed. He was a big distributor of sour mash, he had a devoted manager to run his plant, and he kept an adorable playmate to play with. A charmed life, and one that he deserved. Well, he had made the investment and the investor was entitled to the rewards.

Yes, and he was lucky, too. Who could be as lucky as he to have a manager like The Mole? First one in in the morning and the last to leave at night, his snout snooping around the plant all day. When Possum suggested he take a little time off, have some fun, he said, "I'm getting all I want out of my work."

And who could be as lucky as he to have all the free time a manager like The Mole afforded him? He had plenty of time to spend with Playmate, and plenty of berries to keep her. He dressed her in the finest finery and took her to the chicest clubs. Together, they made comparative studies of the sour mash of his competitors.

And to mix a little business and pleasure, he contracted for her to advertise his sour mash on TV: "To

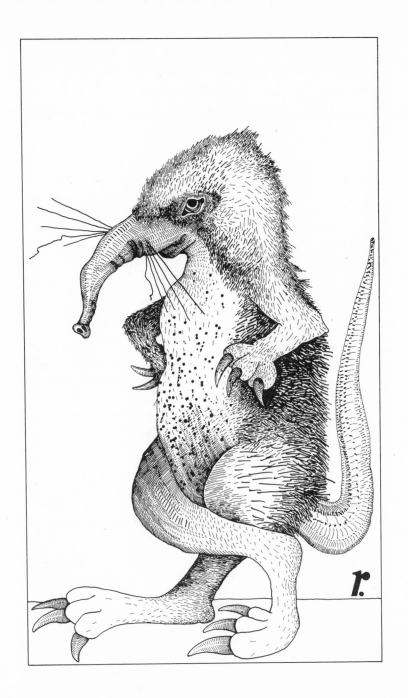

market, to market, to buy mash for a bash," she sang, "you can't go home again without Possum's Sour Mash."

Young and old alike would not go home without Possum's Sour Mash. And business was terrific.

Whenever Possum needed some berries, The Mole gave him some from the vault. Possum wasn't interested in the bottom line. As long as the berries rolled in and The Mole took care of everything, the bottom line would take care of itself.

One unhappy day, the mother of The Mole gnawed on a live wire and lost her ability to gnaw forevermore. Possum said he would mind the plant while The Mole went to pay his respects.

"I'm not going. I'll stay here," said The Mole.

"A mother is entitled to at least a day of mourning," said Possum. "Go!"

"I'm staying out of respect for my mother. She taught me that living is more important. And the plant is my living."

After much urging on Possum's part, The Mole agreed to leave and show his respect. "But just for an hour."

What kind of a son would not mourn his mother for at least a day? wondered Possum. If his mother died, he would give her a day at least, maybe two. Enough of these disturbing thoughts. He would be meeting Playmate in an hour. He needed some berries—berries always made love run smoother. It would be insensitive of him to bother The Mole to get the berries for him on this sad day. He would take the berries himself.

Possum went to the vault. He found the door open. Ah, thought Possum, The Mole was so disturbed about his mother's death that he couldn't take the usual precautions. And he had thought The Mole didn't care;

actually, he just couldn't show his emotions. Possum saw there were very few berries in the vault. That Mole! He was going to surprise his Boss. He made some investments for him. Probably give him the stock certificates on his birthday.

Possum gathered up the few berries, and when he cleaned out the vault, he noticed a door that was ajar at the back of the vault. A door at the back of the vault? Possum didn't know that the vault had that door.

He put his snout through the door to see where it led. By now he was sure he knew where it led—straight to the tunnel that led to the hole in the ground where The Mole made his home.

"And he was such a good worker," said Possum. "First one in in the morning and the last to leave at night."

And what he did in between led him to the slammer for three years.

Now Possum is the first one in in the morning and the last to leave at night.

**MORAL**

**First one in in the morning and the last to leave at night and you can get away with almost anything.**

# TRUST AND SWEAT

"Yesterday, at the break of day, I was in the woods, Mama, and I played with the deer and the geese and there was the soft pure snow and only heaven between us."

"Eat your shredded roots, dear."

"I see marvelous things. I want to write about the things I see." And Shannon told her mother that she was going to fly overseas to the publishing center of the world, and she would write a book and have it published and return home for her publishing party.

"You're just a little sparrow from a one-room schoolhouse. You'll never be able to keep up with the big-city birds, dear. And I hear it's hawk-eat-sparrow there. And you'll starve to death."

"Oh, Mama! I don't have enough meat on my bones for the hawks. And I can't starve. Berries are growing at the sides of the roads there just waiting for me to pick them." And she pecked her mother lovingly and flew off.

Shannon had studied only with trusting sparrows. She found her class was made up mostly of mockingbirds. She trembled when she heard some of the things these mockers said:

158

"There's no place for talent in the market place today."

"There's no place for good writing."

"It's not what you know. It's who you know."

"And even if you get published, they make sure they are in the berries and they let you starve."

Shannon saw that the mockingbirds spent most of their time mocking and little of their time writing. "I don't care how many mockingbirds there are," the little sparrow peeped to herself. "The more there are, the less competition I will have in the market place. Besides, I made this journey to study with Betty Wise, not with the mockingbirds." Betty was the wise owl who worked in publishing. Shannon would trust her teacher, listen to her, listen to her eight times as hard as the mockers did.

Doing things eight times was not new for Shannon. In her class at the one-room schoolhouse, she had heard her lessons in the first grade and she heard them again in the second, then in the third, fourth, and fifth. By the time she reached the eighth grade she understood them thoroughly.

So when Shannon heard Betty say, "Write one page a day," she wrote eight.

"Read an hour a day." She read eight hours.

"Find your own voice." She found she had eight voices and used them all.

"Find out who is buying your kind of story." She bought eight trade publications and found out.

"You have to be ready to sacrifice. Your writing comes first." She skipped meals. She sent beaux on their way. She wouldn't take the time to bring up nestlings.

"Use original sources." She studied the creatures she wrote about in their natural habitat.

Occasionally, she would fly about for exercise. But this did not take time away from her work, for as she flew about she developed her thoughts and wrote them down as soon as she returned to her desk.

By the time her last class was held Shannon finished her book. She submitted it to a publisher who specialized in creatures of the bird and animal world. She had learned who that publisher was, of course, by studying the trade publications. She submitted her manuscript "over the transom" and became the discovery of the spring season. Her book, *Love and Lust in the Forest*, became a bestseller and Shannon made enough berries from it to take care of herself for life.

"She must have slept with *National Geographic*," said the mockers.

"Thank God the hawks didn't get you," said Mama. "How did you do it?"

"It was easy, Mama," she said. "A birdie taught me how."

## MORAL

Some wise birds out there may be telling you how to get what you want. Don't let the mockers keep their teachings from reaching you.

# EXTERNAL
# ATTRACTION

Selma looked at her reflection in the water and squealed, "Why me?" She had feelings like other chimpanzees, a heart like other chimpanzees, the desire to love and be loved in return. But with a face like hers, with its tiny ears and mouth, and her ugly straight legs, all the males ready to mate passed her by.

Her rejection pained her so that she wouldn't go to the watering holes that the young chimps went to. She went only where the old ones went to exchange tales of their conquests of long ago.

And here one day, at the Old Soaks Bar, she heard: "Hello, love of my life."

Selma turned to see who this young male was talking to. Could he be addressing Grandma Gertie? It didn't seem so. She turned back to finish her drink.

"You! I mean you! Will you marry me?" Then, "By the way, what's your name?"

A cruel joke, she thought. "The nut hatch is a few trees down. Or, if you want to swing, go to any palm on First Row."

161

# EXTERNAL ATTRACTION

"I love you and I want to marry you," he said. "My name is Prince Chimp. What's yours?"

Joke or not, it was the first time Selma was asked for her paw in marriage and who knew but that it might be the last. She wouldn't throw in a monkey wrench. He asked her—she would give the answer she had prepared to give since she was a juvenile. "Yes. I love you from the bottom of my heart. I am Selma."

And what a marriage it was! When they went for their walks, they held paws tenderly or Prince Chimp would wrap his tail about Selma's waist. They kissed and embraced for all to see. Romantically, he put the food in her little mouth. He brought her twigs as symbols of his love.

Yet Selma never felt secure of her prince's love. Someday, she feared, he would wake up and see who he had really married.

"Prince, dear, how did you know you loved me?" she asked him one day.

"I just knew," he replied.

"But the male animal is so external in his attraction to the female. Did you see inside me?"

"Baby, I'm as external as any male in my taste. I bought what I saw."

Selma rushed to the nearest pond to look at her reflection. Did her ears grow? Maybe they weren't as small as she thought they were. When she tilted her head and held it closer to the water it did look larger and maybe that was the way the prince saw them. And if she forced her knees apart, she might consider herself a little bowlegged. No. She might as well face the truth. She was ugly. If Prince wanted to be kind to her she wouldn't force him to be cruel. She would never bring up that question again. To change the subject, she asked:

162

# EXTERNAL ATTRACTION

"I was wondering, Prince, what was your first mate like?"

"A beauty."

So this subject is worse, thought Selma. She rested her head on her breast so her flaws wouldn't be so obvious.

"Then why did you leave her?" she asked.

"She had the roundest head, the largest ears, and the most bowed legs of any swinger. And what a swinger she turned out to be. I never knew which troop of chimps she was servicing while I was out in the jungle. You can call me Prince Chump—she took me for every banana I had. With you, my princess, I bought what I saw. No trysts. No chance of trysts. A female just for me."

Selma grinned, confident now that no female chimp could ever take her place.

**MORAL**

**Love is in the needs of the beholder.**

# BOSS

"We work all day gathering the nectar, gathering the pollen, gathering water and resins. We do everything for the benefit of one bee, the queen. And what do we get in return? A little bit of nourishment. A cell in a crowded hive. We bust our wings working, but when we're old we have to beg for a sip of honey." So Worker, a worker bee, left the hive to publish a newspaper that would tell of these injustices. Her paper would make other workers aware of how they were being exploited. It would offer suggestions as to how to right these wrongs.

Honeybee read about all these injustices in *The Daily Buzz*. They were the very injustices she was suffering. Ah, how boldly Worker told of the plight of the worker bees. How courageous she was. How wonderful it would be to work for this fighter for justice. "May I join you?" she asked Worker. So Honeybee left the hive to work for Worker on *The Daily Buzz*.

But alas, Honeybee found that Worker wasn't Worker any more. Worker was now Boss. She had a product to sell. She had a profit to make. She couldn't afford a loss, for a loss could mean she would be in danger of losing her newspaper and she would have no place to go. She wouldn't be welcome at the hive any longer, nor would she want to return.

In her editorials Boss still advocated that the workers get a fairer share of the honey, and she still advocated that they have better living conditions and more power. But she learned overnight that the honey she did not share left more honey in her own honeybag, and that a full day's work on *her* worker's part was necessary to keep her in clover.

"Do you know, my dear Honeybee," said Boss, "that you are supposed to give a full hour's work for an hour's pay?"

*This* from Boss, formerly Worker, fighter for a fair shake for all workers? Honeybee's psyche was shaken by this betrayal. "I bust my wings for *The Daily Buzz*, Boss," she said.

"I clocked you this morning and that's a lot of beeswax. You are flitting about unproductively thirty-five percent of the time. You're just plain loafing forty percent of the time. And only twenty-five percent of the time did I find you working."

Honeybee knew she had been as busy as any bee all day. And now she was disturbed by the many injustices that were heaped upon her. These injustices were just as unjust as the injustices that had caused her to leave the queen's hive in the first place. They were the same injustices she wrote about day and night. She would not tolerate them. She would leave *The Daily Buzz*. But she couldn't go back to the hive again, so she would start her own paper. There she would be able to expose the injustices in the world outside—*The Daily Buzz*—as well as the injustices inside the beehive.

And she left *The Daily Buzz* and started *The Morning Bizz*. And she enticed one of the worker bees to join her. And Honeybee was no longer a worker. She became

Businessbee and made the bee who worked for her bust her wings in the service of *The Morning Bizz*.

And thus is the way of all bosses, no matter what their origins.

**MORAL**

**Workers have to work and bosses have to boss. And one can change one's role but never this rule.**

# THE UGLY DUCKLING— WITH APOLOGIES

Daphne was a duckling and, believe me, she was ugly. She looked at her reflection in the pond one day and the image she saw made her regurgitate like a Strasbourg goose.

Mama Duck realistically evaluated her ugly offspring. "Daphne, you'd better train for a career," said Mama Duck. "I won't be around to take care of you forever, and there's no duck around who'll throw you a fish."

While other ducks were learning how to preen their feathers, Daphne went to the Duck School of Engineering, Architecture, and Business Administration to learn how to build a better nest.

"I want to see the prince," Daphne said to the guard of the royal nest one morning.

"We don't need any," said the guard.

"I have something to tell the prince that will change his life," said Daphne. "I demand to see the prince."

The prince asked what all the quacking was about.

169

# THE UGLY DUCKLING—WITH APOLOGIES

"I can teach you how to build a permanent nest," said Daphne, "so you can have more time to run around with wild ducks."

The prince hardly listened. Every duck tried to sell him everything.

". . . so you can have more time to run around with wild ducks," she repeated.

Ah, thought the prince, this ugly one presents an idea I *want* to buy.

The prince and Daphne worked on the new nest together. They carried the lime together, and the sand, and the water. They cheered each other on when the mixture held together. Daphne blew cotton balls through the walls with the elk's antler the prince found in the woods. They cried together when the new paint washed away in the summer rain. They laughed when they found that the solar-heating system heated the nest.

The mortar of their toil bound them together.

"Will you be my poopsie-woopsie?" asked the prince.

How did the ugly one trap the prince when duckier ducks failed? Some say it was know-how.

**MORAL**

**Cement cements.**

# BREAD

There was a mother hen who lived in a shoe. She had so many chickens she didn't know what to do, so she gave them some broth without any bread, and whipped them all soundly and put them to bed.

"I'm getting out of here, Ma," said Arty. "Do you know what it does to my psyche to get whipped all the time? And can you imagine how it feels to be put to bed by you? Not to mention my energy level! How can I get along without bread? No bread, no Arty." And he took a container of broth and went on his way.

"I guess I'll find a shoe to live in," he cock-a-doodle-dooed bravely.

"No," he cock-a-doodle-dooed more bravely, "I'll build my own shoe. But how do I build a shoe?"

He asked the Wise Old Hen.

"Go down to Shoe Lane and ask the expert shoe-builders," she said.

He went to Shoe Lane and came upon a dazzling shoe made of velvet and cloth-of-gold.

"How can I build a shoe?" he asked Mesmer Eyes.

"Easy," he said. "You take half-cloth and put a little stardust in your eyes and the stardust will show you the

171

way." Arty was not sure, however, that a velvet and cloth-of-gold shoe was his style. He would search further.

He went further down Shoe Lane and came upon a boot of leather with a square toe, a high tongue, and a big silver buckle.

"How can I build a shoe?" he asked Efficiency Cock.

"Take a solid material, work fast, and pick a design that will fit in with your neighbors'." Arty studied Efficiency's shoe. It seemed too pedestrian for him.

He walked a little further and came upon a felt shoe of many colors that reached a fantastic height. The shoe was a little run-down at the heel.

Cock Orpheus responded to his question most co-operatively. "Dream of the image and the pattern will come to you. Find your own material and listen to your own cock-a-doodle-doo."

"That's for me," said Arty. And he went down by the river bed and he dreamed of the image. And the pattern did come to him. And he listened to his own cock-a-doodle-doo and his own cock-a-doodle-doo told him what material to use. He found the hide of a goat, and ribbons, and bells. And Arty made his own handsome shoe.

"I made it! I made it!" He cock-a-doodle-dooed with joy. "With my own dream, and my own image, and my own pattern, and material, and cock-a-doodle-doo, *I made it.*"

And he went into his own shoe, and it felt good.

He drank some broth from his container, and he felt good—for a while.

And then he heard his cock-a-doodle-doo again. And he listened to his cock-a-doodle-doo again. And he heard a rumbling sound. And the sound came from the pit of his stomach. "I want bread!" he cock-a-doodle-dooed.

And he closed his eyes and he dreamed of bread. And the pattern of bread came to him. And he sketched bread

with his claw on the wall of his shoe. And he heard his own cock-a-doodle-doo and it still made a rumbling sound and the sound still came from the pit of his stomach.

"I want bread!" he cock-a-doodle-dooed. "I want bread! I want bread! I want bread!" he cock-a-doodle-dooed again and again and again.

But still no bread.

The experts had been helpful to him before. Perhaps they could help him now.

"How do you get bread?" he asked Mesmer Eyes.

"Well, sometimes you throw stardust in the eyes of young chicks and they get their folks to come across with the bread."

"Not for me," said Arty.

He asked Efficiency.

"That's a problem," he said. "I have to do a little moonlighting here and there. And my bread never seems to rise at the same rate as the cost of living, but I'm not starving yet."

Perhaps Cock Orpheus:

"If you find out how to make bread tell me. I'm still trying to find out," he said.

Arty had spoken to the experts, but he still didn't know how to make bread. It was time for him to go back to see the Wise Old Hen.

"I listened to your advice," he said. "I went to see the experts. You should see the handsome shoe I built. You must come to see it. Any time. But I need bread and I asked the experts how to make it. They don't know any more about making bread than I do."

"You went to the experts? What experts did you go to?" asked the Wise Old Hen."

# BREAD

"You know. The experts. Mesmer Eyes. Efficiency Cock. Cock Orpheus."

"Shoemakers?" The Wise Old Hen cackled. She rolled on the ground. "If you want to make shoes, you ask a shoemaker. But if you want to know how to make bread ask—a baker."

And she cackled a wise old cackle, and cock-a-doodled a wise cockle-doodle-doo, and started to hobble away.

"Wait," called Arty. "Where can I find an expert baker?"

"There are many around. But there is a special knack in handling the dough and it's not easily taught."

## MORAL

It's often easier to make a shoe than to make bread.

# THE MEISTERSINGER

Clara was a cuckoo bird. "Cuck-koo, cuck-koo, cuck-koo," she sang. She was a sad cuckoo but she wanted to be glad. "There are many glad birds," she thought, "and I would rather be glad. What can I do to make me feel glad? And she thought. "I know what I'll do. I'll change my song." And she threw her neck back and pointed her beak to the skies. She tried some high notes. And she played around with her rhythm.

"You sing with soul," said her ma. "Ask the Meistersinger."

"You sing with new rhythm," said the Meister. "Smoothe out the rough spots. You can be a professional."

"Not me," said Clara. "I'm just a cuckoo bird who wants to change her song." And Clara worked with the Meister and she developed her song. She polished it. She gave it a finish. And when changing her song, Clara hardly felt sad at all.

"You're ready for the Sanctuary Songfest," said the Meister. "You sing like a canary."

"Not me," said Clara. "Cuckoo birds do not sing in the Songfest." But deep in her secret heart she wanted to

sing in the Songfest. No matter that she was just a cuckoo. No matter that she had cooed her song many a summer like a cuckoo. Maybe if she sang like a canary at the Songfest, she would not feel sad, and maybe she would be sent on missions to the Audubon Society to focus their Spring Campaign on the much-maligned cuckoo bird, and maybe . . . . "Not me," she said again.

"Why don't you check with Mockingbird?" said the Meister. "He is a fine critic."

"Phnyeh! You sing phnyeh," said Mockingbird. "You do not follow the rules. Poor phrasing. At which school did you matriculate? You do not soar untrammeled into the realms of beauty. You are a dud."

"But the Meister said . . ."

"He is an excellent critic, but in this matter he is a dodo."

Clara felt crushed. "I guess that's the answer," she said. "I sing phnyeh. You are the expert. You should know."

"Why don't you sing your song any more?" asked the Meister.

"Because I sing phnyeh. Mockingbird said so. And I know so. And ask any bird in the woods and he will tell you I sing phnyeh."

"But you have your own song and you're good. Come meet some songbirds who have made it. *And keep singing.*"

"I'll try," said Clara. "I promise. I will be a good cuckoo and I'll practice my new songs."

But Clara did not try. She went back to her tree and sang her old sad song.

The Meister came to call. "Come to our Seminar for Creative Songbirds," he said.

"I have no song to sing," she chirped.

"Then come and listen. Talk to other songbirds—it will be good for you. You know there is such a thing known as songbird's block. But only a creative bird can have this block. So you must be a creative bird."

"My song is phnyeh, but I will come anyway."

And she went to the seminar. And she heard the Meister say, "If you dream, and sing, and practice to improve each day, any creative bird can become a professional. Even a cuckoo can learn to sing like a canary."

"Ha!" laughed Blue-Winged Goose. "A cuckoo sing like a canary!"

"He-haw," laughed Donkeybird, "maybe a cowbird can sing like a canary, too."

"Or a jackass," said Cowbird.

"Hear, hear!" said the Meister. And all the birds laughed.

Clara looked about her in dismay. How could these rude birds hurt the Meister? Some bird should stop them. But who could stop them? Not I. If I get in front of them and sing they'll all look at me and I'll die. I'll simply die. But what other bird can prove the Meister is right? I'm the only cuckoo here. . . .

"Listen to the Meis?" said Sillybird. "He's selling his soul for a few worms!"

Clara could bear it no longer. "Wait," she heard herself say, "I can prove it."

And Clara began to sing. She sang of sadness. She sang of joy. She sang of love requited and she sang of love lost. She sang from her heart. She sang her own song. She sang like a cuckoo who sang like . . . .

"Like a canary," cackled Blue-Winged Goose.

"Like a canary," purred Donkeybird.

"Like a canary," mooed Cowbird.

"Like a canary," giggled Sillybird.

# THE MEISTERSINGER

There were catcalls from the catbirds and whistles from the whistlers. Clara got goose bumps all over. "He did it!" sang Clara as she raised the Meister's left wing so he could take a bow with her. "He did it because he believed in me."

"How can I do it, too?" asked Minibird.

"Believe, believe good things birds say about you for they may be as true, or possibly more so, as the bad."

Now Clara is glad, as glad as any bird can be.

## MORAL

Believe good things others say about you. They may be as true, or possibly more so, as the bad.

# CEREBRA

Pulchritude was a crane with a long bill and a small head. "Thank God you have my looks," said her mother. "At least you'll find someone to marry you. With your pinhead of a brain you'd never be able to learn enough to earn your own keep."

Pulchritude found a mate who wanted her only for her beauty. So when her breast began to sag, he went off with a sleeker mate.

Pulchritude was very unhappy. "My mother should have made me go to school. I am alone in the world now. My sex appeal is gone and what can I do? Sure, I can dip my bill in the water and pick up a fish here and there, but that is living from bill to mouth." She told her friends her tale of woe, and after many tears decided she would try to improve her lot. She would see a certified adviser who would be able to give her the professional advice that would help bring about a change.

Every day she dipped her bill in the sea. The first fish she caught she brought to Cerebra. If she was lucky enough to catch another fish, she ate that day. Many a day she did not eat at all. It was a sacrifice, but she was sure it was worth it. She would get advice that would make her life different. She was beginning to feel happy already in anticipation of the very professional advice she would get that would make her life different.

For seventy-five days, Pulchritude brought a fish each day to Cerebra's office. At last she had paid the fee for her planned visit. She had made many sacrifices, but was sure all the effort she had put into getting the fish and bringing them to Cerebra would be worthwhile.

"I came to you because you are a certified adviser," she said to Cerebra, "and I want the professional advice that only a certified adviser can give me." And she told her tale of woe.

Cerebra seemed astonished when Pulchritude told her that her mother said she had a pinhead-sized brain. "Why, your brain is no smaller than mine," she said.

When Pulchritude told her that her mate had left because her breast sagged, she was appropriately appalled. She nodded her head in sympathy when Pulchritude told her how unhappy she was, and at times cocked her head as though pondering Pulchritude's problems deeply.

After listening for forty-two minutes, Cerebra said, "Now I will give you my advice. My advice is: Go to school."

"That is your advice? Go to school?"

"Yes. Go to school. Get a certificate and you can have a career that will bring you more fish. Today a good career even gives you sex appeal."

Pulchritude was enraged. "What kind of advice is that?" she croaked. "I didn't even go to night school and I give my friends the same advice you give me."

"But, my dear, there is a difference."

"What is the difference? I fail to see the difference."

"The difference, my dear, is seventy-five fish. I get it and you don't."

## MORAL

Schooling pays.

# THE BEAVER AND
# THE SLOTH

Elmer was a sloth, a lazy sloth, a son-of-a-lazy sloth. He walked upside down, hanging from the branches, and he slept upside down with his claws hooked into the branches of the trees. Sometimes, when he was hanging in a tree, a parrot would fly by and call, "Are you dead yet?" It would take a while but he would respond, "No." And then, after a pause, "Not yet." Another pause: "Not yet, I think." Elmer knew that many a sloth hung from a limb totally dead. But it hardly mattered to him or any other creature, for even when the sloth was alive his state was hardly different.

Now Elmer had been living his death-in-life for many a year. And he had watched the leopards running about quite energetically. And he had watched the ants busily working. And the tigers running off for their kill. And they all seemed to live at a level of excitement he had never experienced. What was it all about? he wondered. What was he missing? He would like—oh, there he went nodding off again, he would fight it—he would like to find out what this busyness was all about.

The thought so stirred within him that it kept him

awake. Of course, he could ask a fellow sloth, but he felt that if he got up the energy to ask one, he would find that that sloth knew as little about work as he did. No, he couldn't learn how to be energetic from a lazy creature like himself. He would have to learn from a busy creature. He nodded off again and now welcomed his slumber, for he had earned it: He had thought a remarkable thought.

One would think that such remarkable thinking would entitle him to some peace and quiet. Entitled or not, he wasn't getting it. Cutting through his dreams, he heard the sounds of the chipping of wood and of feet scurrying hurriedly about, and then a squeaky voice saying, "How does he do it? How?"

There was no point in trying to sleep now. Elmer would have to put an end to this disturbance. *"How* does *who* do *what?"* he grunted.

"My card," said the creature. And what a strange-looking creature he was with his webbed hind feet and his flat, broad tail. 'William Beaver, builder of dams and lodges,' read the card. "You look at me as if you have never seen a creature like me before. You probably haven't. I have traveled a long distance, from the northern woods to this tropical forest, just to meet you."

Interesting. Anyone who traveled a long distance just to meet him could possibly be worth his staying awake. He would force his eyes to stay open and try to concentrate.

The beaver squeaked, "On the day I was born, my father called me Billy and by nightfall said, 'Enough of this fooling around, William. It's time you did a little work.' Since the night of the day of my birth, I've been working my claws to the bone and I've been happy to do so. I like to work. A beaver is a worker. If he is not that, he is nothing. There is nothing I'd rather be doing than working."

## THE BEAVER AND THE SLOTH

Elmer was annoyed. Did this visitor come to him to lecture him on the virtues of working? He had thought he might like to find out what work was all about. But how did this beaver know? "What has this got to do with me?" he asked.

The beaver squeaked on. "Lately things haven't been going well for me. The waters that I live in are polluted. With volcanoes erupting and earthquakes quaking, all my foundations are cracking. My son doesn't want to go into the construction business—he wants to stay in the woods and chop wood. My daughter doesn't believe in blissful matrimony—she just wants to accumulate a male harem. Some of my best friends have been taken to Our Maker. My tail hurts so that I can hardly sit on it. I know only how to work, and my doctor says I must have a complete rest. Now I've been watching you hang from the limb, spaced out to the count of a thousand, with that who-cares attitude—a perfect study in relaxation. I must learn how to relax. But how? I can't seem to get the hang of it. Can you teach me?"

This creature seemed serious. He was asking Elmer for help. He evidently didn't know that no creature ever asked him for help with anything. Well, well. This was an interesting turn of events. "Don't you have any more get-up-and-go?" Elmer asked sympathetically.

William began to bristle. "That's not what I came all the way here for. *I came here to learn how to relax*," he squealed in a most agitated manner.

Elmer saw that William indeed needed to relax. He would try again. In a low, slow, hypnotic voice, he said, "So you came here, Billy, to learn how to relax . . ."

Then Elmer paused. He paused to see whether he was breathing. Then he paused to try to remember what he was thinking before he met this strange creature from a faraway land. And he remembered that he wondered

187

what he was missing by not working. And he chuckled. And he remembered that he was going to ask a busy creature. And he laughed. And he remembered that this beaver who worked like a beaver wanted to learn how to be lazy, just—like—him. Man! That was a laugh. Lazy, just like him! Now he laughed so heartily he fell off his limb. Well, he was an expert and he would give this beaver the best advice a sloth had to offer:

"Ready? Breathe in deep. Breathe out slow. Keep breathing. Then check. You have to feel you have no head on your shoulders and no bite in your teeth. You have to hang loose and let it all hang out. No ties, no bars, but when you get up the energy, a little la-de-da. And this is the most important thing I can tell you— when you get the urge to work, *sit on your tail.*"

And Elmer got back on his limb. And he nodded back to a happy sleep with the happy thought that he had given the beaver the best advice he could possibly give and that he would never have to think about going on that work trip again.

**MORAL**

**Is this trip necessary?**

# AN ELEPHANT NEVER FORGETS

Olga is an elephant. She is old—sixty, if a day.

I am an elephant. I am clever. I am so clever I am clever enough to see that we elephants are a dying species. Après moi. I'm here now. I want a long life. Olga has surpassed the life expectancy of African elephants by ten years so far. I will observe her (unbeknownst to her) and I will do what she does and have a long life. I observe.

Playtime. Other elephants roll the rocks about. Olga kicks the rocks. I kick the rocks. I get sore toes.

Fatso and Blimpo and Dumbo lick my toes with their trunks to comfort me. Olga looks on—with amusement, it seems. Maybe this is it. She conserves her sympathy. I will conserve my sympathy. When Dumbo trips over a dinosaur's carcass, I laugh. It does not make me feel more energetic, or stronger. No, lack of sympathy cannot be the answer. I will observe further.

When other elephants push over the *Acacia tortilis* and eat hundreds of pounds of their leaves, Olga hardly stoops to pick them up with her trunk. I barely eat. My stomach rumbles like the sound of a stampede. It does not make me feel younger. Limiting my caloric intake cannot be the answer. I will observe still further.

Her appendages are no larger or smaller than mine—it cannot be her equipment.

Her skin color is no foggier—it cannot be her color.

She takes long naps leaning to. I take a long nap and a rhinoceros almost kills me.

Big-game photographers come to take our pictures. She runs away. I hide when the *National Geographic* snaps our herd. I am left out of the winter issue and I don't feel one bit better.

This will never do. I will have to ask her. I will have to ask her directly.

"Olga," I ask her, "what do you owe your long life to?"

She grumbles.

"It's no skin off your trunk. You can tell me. I will put in a good word for you after you're gone, and elephants forever after will remember you, if you will only tell me your secret.

"An elephant never forgets a promise," I say.

She takes a deep drag of a smoking weed and snorts.

"A promise?" she asks.

I feel her leaning my way. "A promise," I say.

"An elephant never forgets a promise?" she asks for my word.

I reassure her. "An elephant never forgets a promise," I swear. "Is it a secret herb? Low cholesterol? Special vitamins?"

She grumbles.

"A special mumbo-jumbo?"

That tickles her. "None of that," she says.

"Okay, Olga. Level with me," I say. "What do you owe your long life to?"

# AN ELEPHANT NEVER FORGETS

"Hate," she says.

I think I have not heard her right. I look for a serpent hissing in the grass. And she repeats the word, "Hate." She seems to boost up her energy when she says the word. She raises her trunk as if she scents an enemy in the brush. "Hate! Hate! Hate!" She is all charged up now.

"How do you hate? What do you hate? Why do you hate so much?" I ask. It is hard for me to believe what my ears hear. It is hard for me to believe that what I hear can make for a long elephant life. Is she kidding me? I will have to judge that. I wait for the answer.

"Hate," she says. "I hate my sister Lovey. When I was fifteen, she stole my beau. I promised myself I wouldn't give her the satisfaction of letting her see me die. An elephant never forgets. When she dies, then I will be ready to die. Hate keeps me going."

"Hate?" I say. I don't believe her. Maybe it's her will to outlive. I will have to observe her further.

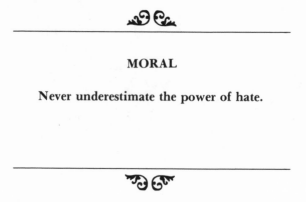

## MORAL

**Never underestimate the power of hate.**

IW
892236

R00126 07494

_JC_

398.245  IW 892236    9 IDA WILLIAMS

AUG 23 1982

Schuman, Beatrice Chernuchin.
  It's not easy to marry an elephant :
and other fables / by Beatrice
Chernuchin Schuman ; illustrated by
Roland Wolff. -- New York : F. Fell,
c1982.
  192 p. : ill. ; 22 cm.

1. Fables.   I. Title

GA    05 AUG 82    8302049   GAPAnc    81-68909